Melville's Confidence Man

Melville's Confidence Man

From Knave to Knight

Tom Quirk

University of Missouri Press
Columbia & London
1982

Copyright © 1982 by
The Curators of the University of Missouri
Library of Congress Catalog Card Number 82-2824
Printed and bound in the United States of America
University of Missouri Press, Columbia, Missouri 65211
All rights reserved

Library of Congress Cataloging in Publication Data

Quirk, Thomas V., 1946-
    Melville's Confidence man.

    Bibliography: p. 167.
    Includes index.
    1. Melville, Herman, 1819-1891.
The confidence-man. I. Title.
PS2384.C63Q5   813'.3   82-2824
ISBN 0-8262-0370-1   AACR2

Poem #1551 by Emily Dickinson is reprinted by
permission of the publishers and the Trustees of
Amherst College from The Poems of Emily Dickinson,
edited by Thomas H. Johnson, Cambridge, Mass.: The
Belknap Press of Harvard University Press, Copyright
1951, © 1955, 1979 by the President and Fellows of
Harvard College.

The Bingham drawings are reproduced
courtesy of the people of Missouri.

In Memory of
Henrietta Howard
and for
Leon Howard

Acknowledgments

The genesis and preparation of this book owe much to many people, and my debts are gladly acknowledged. With the help of Leon Howard, George Arms, and James Barbour, I was able to clarify and fortify my argument and to profit from their better judgment and generous encouragement from the very beginning. Leon Howard warrants special mention. He taught me, both by patient instruction and by living example, the humanizing value of simple and honest curiosity. He followed my uneven progress with sympathy and interest, and his suggestions were always helpful and encouraging. It is enough to say, I suppose, that the partial dedication of this book to him is an insufficient token of my gratitude.

Other thanks are due as well. I am grateful to the University of Missouri Research Council for a grant to pay the cost of typing the manuscript. I am also indebted to Harrison Hayford for allowing me to see the Northwestern-Newberry edition of *The Confidence-Man* in page proofs so that I might bring my own citations into line with the definitive edition of the novel. I am also grateful to Professor Hayford for his concrete and fruitful suggestions concerning style and format. Finally, I must thank Robert Sattelmeyer, who went over the manuscript with me and suggested improvements in tone and argument.

I must thank my wife and daughter as well. This book was written during stolen hours—stolen not, I am confident, from my teaching and administrative responsibilities, but from my family. For my wife's encouragement and indulgence and for my young daughter's uncomprehending but reliable good nature, I am particularly grateful. They did not begrudge me the theft.

T.Q.
March 1982
Columbia, Missouri

Contents

George Caleb Bingham, *Country Politician*, 1849.
Nelson Gallery—Atkins Museum (Nelson Fund).

Introduction

If I have understood this book aright, it
proves two things beyond shadow or question:
1. That Christianity is the very invention
of Hell itself; 2. & that Christianity is the
(most) precious and elevating and enobling
boon ever vouchsafed to the world.

Mark Twain's marginal comment in his copy of
W. E. H. Lecky's History of European Morals.[1]

Those—dying then,
Knew where they went—
They went to God's Right Hand—
That Hand is amputated now
And God cannot be found—

The abdication of Belief
Makes the Behavior small—
Better an ignis fatuus
Than no illume at all—[2]

Emily Dickinson

In 1947, Richard Chase declared that Melville's *The
Confidence-Man: His Masquerade* is a "great book,"
and, two years later, that it was Melville's "second-best
achievement."[3] Since these proclamations, if not before,
this last novel published during Melville's lifetime has
received increasing attention and respect from scholars
and critics alike. If finally Chase's reasons for supposing
the greatness of this novel are somewhat idiosyncratic
and his interpretation of the book far from compelling,
he nevertheless delivered a judgment that more and more
readers and critics were to eventually share. There have
been, of course, dissenters. Many have found the novel
not simply confusing, but confused. They believe it chaotic, fragmented, truncated—random invective by an
author whose own bitterness had depleted his talents.

1

For those admirers of the book who would counter these claims, clearly the task was to demonstrate a sustained imaginative coherence that justified its felt greatness.

Virtually from the beginning of the twentieth-century revaluation of *The Confidence-Man*, the satirical qualities of the book have been recognized, but the specificity of simple social satire would seem to preclude an examination of those ampler and deeper dimensions of Melville's special genius present in most of his novels and so remarkable in *Moby-Dick*. Thus, the temptation to view the book not simply as satire but as satirical allegory proved to be a strong one, for the allegorical development of a narrative has as its necessary foundation a lower layer of disguised but identifiable and ultimately more significant meanings.

Among the several allegorical interpretations of *The Confidence-Man*, a discernible group of critics has provided the ablest and most thorough interpretation, one that has been described as the "standard line of interpretation."[4] Foremost among them is Elizabeth Foster, whose 1954 Hendricks House edition of the novel provided indispensable notes to the text and a long and provocative introduction attempting to deal with the book as a narrative whole; she cogently promoted the view that this novel should be viewed as a satirical allegory in which the confidence man is a manifestation of Satan. Foster and a number of other critics hold that the title character is the Devil in masquerade, a figure whose swindles, by dint of the swindler's primal, evil nature, have a cosmic significance that transcends the level of social satire. Moreover, this allegorical view is appealing because it enables readers to reconcile many of the apparent inconsistencies of the book and provides a rather precise means of evaluating the moral disposition of those passengers aboard the *Fidèle* victimized by the confidence man.

The present study, though it unquestionably benefits from the studies of Foster and others, nevertheless disputes this allegorical interpretation of the book. It seemed unreasonable to believe that Melville could achieve the sort of detachment necessary for pure allegory and still create a "great" book. Throughout his career, Melville's special genius normally required a good deal of involvement with his material, especially in his profounder books; and this involvement was typically attended by vacillations of thought and feeling toward and artistic ambition for his subject matter. Implicit in the notion that Melville's title character possesses a fixed symbolic significance is the equal assumption that the author's attitude toward his subject, and especially toward his own created character, was also fixed and that he meant merely to articulate deep-seated and inflexible attitudes toward his society and its prevailing mores and religious convictions. But the author, who had more than once embarked on a "chartless voyage" in his fiction and, in fact, had typically done so in his more serious books, was unlikely, it seemed to me, to adopt with any success a mode of creation that called for the calculated articulation of ideas rather than the probing discovery and gradual unfolding of the richness of his material. Certainly, his creative imagination had been flexible in *Mardi*, *Moby-Dick*, and *Pierre*, and, I suspected, became so in *The Confidence-Man*.

Moreover, the pervasive and generally recognized ambiguity of this book, it seems clear, could scarcely have proceeded solely from an ambition to disguise a sacrilegious intent. It surely developed as well out of an authentic ambivalence. Melville had been genuinely fascinated by what he would come to call in *Billy Budd* the "moral emergency," and what he had called in *Pierre* "the ambiguities"—he had pressed such an emergency upon the guileless Pierre, had explored it in such short stories as "Bartleby the Scrivener" and "The Lightning-Rod Man," and would dramatize it in *Billy Budd*. I did not think it probable that he would have abandoned this ethical and psychological curiosity in *The Confidence-Man*, especially when the blunt appeals for confidence made by his title character instantly posed just such a moral predicament for would-be dupes. Though Melville himself might have been incapable of religious faith, to make his pilgrims aboard the *Fidèle* repeated victims of a "Devil's Joke" would indeed, as Emily Dickinson recognized, make "Behavior small"—small for the author as well as his characters.

Though genuine admiration for the book and its author no doubt prompted an allegorical view of *The Confidence-Man*, I felt it did neither justice. Melville often brought his characters into collision with a moral dilemma, not in order to vent his spleen, but to explore the human personality and the "queer, unaccountable caprices" of the "natural heart," as he put it in this novel.[5] The voice of a fine moral intelligence such as Melville's is most stimulating not when it artfully disguises a clear intention, but when it struggles for original and ambitious literary embodiment.

This study, then, attempts to explain how such a curious book as *The Confidence-Man* might have come to be written. The mode of its composition was clearly of a different sort than that used in his other books, a method Melville himself had suggested in the famous "Agatha letters" to Hawthorne in 1852. More significantly, the creative process described there can be brought to bear upon other sorts of evidence related to the genesis of the novel, allowing for reasonable speculation about how the author's attitudes and interest grew and changed during the development of his subject.

As a genetic study, this book seeks to trace the contours of *The Confidence-Man* as they probably developed in the author's creative imagination. This approach enables one to trace the author's deepening interest and involvement in his subject and also reveals the genuinely high literary ambitions Melville eventually had for his title character. A part of this process involves locating the personal element in the book and identifying the skeptical but humane state of mind that Melville achieved in the latter stages of its composition, causing him to transform his confidence man from a simple knave to a sort of knight-errant of confidence. A consideration of Melville's aspirations as realized in the novel leads me to argue that the book possesses a greater thematic and imaginative coherence than even the book's most ardent apologists have identified. I have attempted to take into account all the verifiable facts about the composition of the book, but the absence of plentiful evidence has often forced me to be more speculative than I would have liked. Additionally, the organization of my study is to some extent artificial, since the social and religious and literary "significances" (to use Melville's term) that the author discovered in the development of his narrative probably did not occur to him in so discrete and neatly sequential a way as the structure of this book may suggest. Nevertheless, Melville's movement from bitter and narrow satire and antireligious feelings to high literary ambition and deeply felt human sympathy, which I trace in the following chapters, makes for a more familiar picture of Herman Melville and, I hope, for a better book than even its most enthusiastic admirers have described.

George Caleb Bingham, *Weary Traveler*, ca. 1849.
The St. Louis Art Museum.

Chapter 1

Significances

In chapter 44 of *The Confidence-Man*, Melville briefly speculated on the nature of original characters in fiction and implied that he hoped his confidence man approached, even if he did not achieve the originality of those characters in Shakespeare, Cervantes, and Milton about whom he speculated. Melville does not give such authors credit for inventing their most original characters, however. On the contrary, he argued that they were based on extensive observation and good luck:

> But for new, singular, striking, odd, eccentric, and all sorts of entertaining and instructive characters, a good fiction may be full of them. To produce such characters, an author, beside other things, must have seen much, and seen through much: to produce but one original character, he must have had much luck.
>
> There would seem but one point in common between this sort of phenomenon in fiction and all other sorts: it cannot be born in the author's imagination—it being as true in literature as in zoology, that all life is from the egg. (239)

More importantly, however, in chapter 44 Melville indicates where such original characters, and characters in general, are to be found:

> Where does any novelist pick up any character? For the most part, in town, to be sure. Every great town is a kind of man-show, where the novelist goes for his stock, just as the agriculturist goes to the cattle-show for his. But in the one fair, new species of quadrupeds are hardly more rare, than in the other are new species of characters—that is, original ones. (238)

This was a new approach to fiction for Melville, whose

7

earlier romances (except for the recent *Israel Potter*) were autobiographical or, in the cases of *Mardi* and *Moby-Dick*, seemingly so. Yet it was an approach he had been meditating for at least the four years since 12 August 1852, when he wrote Nathaniel Hawthorne about an anecdote he had heard on a recent visit to Nantucket that had aroused in him such a lively interest that he had asked the teller, a New Bedford lawyer named John Clifford, to send him the full story. The document arrived a few days after his return to Pittsfield. It was an account of a Falmouth woman, Agatha Robertson, who had waited patiently for seventeen years for the return of the husband who had deserted her shortly after their marriage. Melville had not, as Clifford supposed, planned to make immediate "literary use" of it himself; but, after reading the complete account, he turned the subject over in his mind as the possible foundation for "a regular story" and decided that it was more in Hawthorne's vein than in his. Accordingly, he sent his friend the manuscript he had received from Clifford along with some of his own observations about it and other related observations he had made on his trip.[1]

Hawthorne was, at the most, uncertain about undertaking the project and never did so; and Melville, probably in November 1852, asked him to return the manuscript and add anything that may have occurred to him during his "random thinking" about the material so that Melville could "endeavor to do justice to so interesting a story of reality."[2] He may have worked on it during the following winter, but if he did, the result, if it survives, has not been recovered. The original letter to Hawthorne, however, is an important document because it shows how Melville went about extrapolating the story of a real person into a work of fiction and provides a basis for considering other evidence about his approach to the most puzzling of all his later books, *The Confidence-Man.*

Melville had a natural relish and respect for the "fact"— either the fact of his own personal experience or a doc-

umented account of some remarkable event. It was customary with him to supplement and graft upon his own
autobiographical romances factual material garnered from
books, especially travel narratives and documentary studies. Part of his motive in writing *Mardi*, he claimed, was
to establish by contrast the truth of *Typee* and *Omoo*,
which had been researched as well as experienced. In
1851 Melville was delighted to learn from Evert Duyckinck
of the actual sinking of the *Ann Alexander* by a whale,
for the documented account verified what he had written in *Moby-Dick*. For Melville, this whale was an irre-
futable "Commentator" on the truth of his novel.[3] Similarly, what may have first interested Melville in the
Agatha story was the way it validated his recent treatment of the abandoned fiancée, Lucy Tartan, in *Pierre*.[4]
And later Melville was to base *Israel Potter* and "Benito
Cereno" upon documentary evidence that provided the
author, as the Agatha story had done, "a skeleton of
actual reality to build about with fulness & veins &
beauty."[5]

In offering the story to Hawthorne, Melville mentioned
certain "tributary items" that he had collected in his
visit to the Elizabeth Islands, the actual scene of the
Agatha story. Among these items were a "high cliff over-
hanging the sea & crowned with a pasture for sheep," a
lighthouse, and a post box, "a little rude wood box with
a lid to it & a leather hinge."[6] In mentioning the specific
elements of a recent experience, Melville's mind moved
readily from concrete images to their symbolic suggestions. He advised Hawthorne that a sheep atop the cliff
should wander to the very edge of the precipice and thus
cast a shadow upon the beach a hundred feet below and
send its "mild innocent glance far out upon the water."
In this "strange and beautiful contrast," Melville believed, "we have the innocence of the land placidly eyeing
the malignity of the sea." Such a scene would symbolically prefigure the encounter of the innocent Agatha
and her "sea-lover." In like manner, the post box seemed
to have an intrinsic symbolic significance: "Owing to

the remoteness of the lighthouse from any settled place no regular <male> mail reaches it."[7] And Melville remarked that, after her abandonment, Agatha should daily go to this box for seventeen years in anticipation of a letter from her lost husband; "as the hopes gradually decay in her, so does the post itself & the little box decay."[8]

In making these suggestions to Hawthorne, Melville advised his friend rather boldly on how to write the Agatha story. But he excused what may have appeared a bit of "strange impertinent officiousness" on the grounds that "these things do, in my mind, seem legitimately to belong to the story; for they were visably suggested to me by scenes I actually beheld while on the very coast where the story of Agatha occurred."[9] And the details from Clifford's diary account of the story that Melville believed should receive special emphasis, such as the three shawls that Robertson sent his daughter after so long an absence, were mentioned in the confidence that Hawthorne would have noted them himself. Melville often confesses in the Agatha letter that Hawthorne, too, will discern the "suggestiveness" of the material, for the Agatha story is *instinct with significance.*[10]

Melville believed that no impertinence was involved in offering these "tributary items" to Hawthorne, for he felt that the significance he had drawn from the material of the story itself and from his visit to the actual scene were intrinsic parts of the whole, and he believed that Hawthorne would accept his suggestions as belonging to the story itself: "I do not therefore, My Dear Hawthorne, at all imagine that you will think I am so silly as to flatter myself I am giving you anything of my own. I am but restoring to you your own property— which you would quickly enough have identified for yourself—had you but been on the spot as I happened to be."[11]

Melville's inclination to extract from the actual event those latent "significances" with which the Agatha story was "instinct" provides a starting point for this study of the author's last full-length novel, *The Confidence-*

Man: His Masquerade (1857), for Melville's imagination
operated in this novel in the same way that it operated
on the Agatha material a few years earlier, a way essentially different from that employed in his earlier books.
Rather than "spin a yarn" based on his own or someone
else's experience, as he had done previously, Melville
composed his novel by developing gradually the significance latent within his title character.

The criminal exploits of the "original" confidence
man, who had been apprehended in New York City in
July 1849, were widely known, and this character provided Melville with a "skeleton of actual reality to build
about." The method he used in fleshing out his fictional
character was generally associative and often symbolic;
and the original confidence man offered a fund of "suggestiveness" from which Melville's creative imagination
drew liberally. To study the novel, then, is to study the
evolving "significances" he found in his title character.

Melville's acquaintance with notices of the original
swindler known as "the confidence man" did not provide immediate inspiration for a book or even a story,
however; newspaper and magazine articles describing
his reemergence (for the same swindler had had his greatest notoriety six years before) appeared in the spring of
1855, but Melville did not begin his novel until that fall.
During the interval between the published accounts of
the capture of the "confidence man," with which Melville was certainly familiar, and his beginning of the
novel itself, he wrote three stories—"The Bell Tower,"
"Jimmy Rose," and "I and My Chimney." All of these
stories are thematically related to one another in their
concern with the debilitating and, in "The Bell Tower,"
devastating effects of pride, a pride the author seems to
have detected in himself and to have deemed unwise
and unprofitable. But they have little in common with
The Confidence-Man in either subject matter or spirit,
for his book would have more to do with the examination of other men's folly than his own.

Melville had displayed his interest in swindles and swindlers at least since the publication of *Redburn* (1849), which is suffused with an atmosphere of chicanery and venality and which includes, among others, a type of confidence man, Pat the Irishman, who diddles the crew of the *Highlander* out of fifteen fathoms of rope and literally "cuts and runs."[12] And in *Moby-Dick* (1851), Stubb hoodwinks the crew of the *Bouton de Rose* and wins the prize of the ambergris hidden within the diseased corpse of their captured whale.[13] More recently, Melville had written a short story based on his own experience with a roguish peddler, "The Lightning-Rod Man" (*Putnam's*, August 1854). But, despite his evident interest in the subject matter and in the exploits of the original confidence man as full of "significance," Melville's ill health probably precluded the possibility of attempting a long piece of fiction that spring, for he had suffered an attack of rheumatism in February, and of sciatica that June.

Ill health also prevented him from participating in a gala fancy dress picnic in early September. Although he was in attendance, he was not in fancy dress; the *Berkshire Eagle*, which noted his attendance, also mentioned that he was "recovering" from a severe illness.[14] Melville was probably identifying his own attitude toward that event in *The Confidence-Man* when he had his cosmopolitan say, "Life is a pic-nic *en costume*. . . . To come in plain clothes, with a long face, as a wiseacre, only makes one a discomfort to himself, and a blot upon the scene" (133). If the reports of an ingenious swindler provided him with his "germ," this fancy dress picnic probably modified his conception of the subject. He adopted a narrative detachment consistent with his evident feelings at that picnic, but he had his central figure dress in costume and pander to the world's folly. He had justified a similar standoffishness, which had characterized his behavior since his health had begun to fail, when he had the narrator of "I and My Chimney" say, "My city friends all wonder why I don't come to see them, as in former times. They think I am getting sour and unsocial. Some say that I have become a sort of mossy old misanthrope, while all the time the fact is I am simply standing guard over my mossy old chimney; for it is resolved between me and my chimney, that I and my chimney will never surrender."[15]

This sort of obstinate determination, at odds with the pleadings of the narrator's family, was in part a false pride. However, though Melville himself had swallowed his pride after the dismal failure of *Pierre* (1852) and had turned his hand to magazine writing, he seems never to have given up the idea of writing novels. He had in fact written *Israel Potter* (1855) for serial publication, though the task could not have proved very challenging to him; for he had promised his publisher that there would be very little "reflective writing" in it, "nothing weighty."[16] And he had assured the Harpers that he could produce a book-length manuscript about "Tortoise Hunting," but this project apparently only resulted in the sketches he eventually sold to *Putnam's* as "The Encantadas."[17] Under different circumstances he might have treated the subject of "Benito Cereno" more expansively; but as it stands, the conclusion to this story seems rushed and truncated, containing as it does what a reader for *Putnam's* described as those "dreary documents at the end."[18] Nevertheless, Melville still seems to have been casting about for a novel-length subject and in August ordered two books from Harpers that might have provided material for another exotic romance.[19] This impulse resulted in no tangible results, but Melville was certainly contemplating another book that fall.

His health evidently improved during the summer, and he was well enough by mid-September to take his mother on a "few days jaunt" to Albany.[20] Before returning home, he purchased in an Albany bookstore a copy of *Don Quixote*, which would eventually have a great deal to do with the novel he began sometime in October, though it is doubtful that he realized it at the time.[21] Rather, his original ambitions for his book were proba-

bly more "magazinish" than profoundly literary. As Leon
Howard has suggested, Melville may have originally intended his book for serialization, in which the adventures of his confidence man could be indefinitely extended as a series of satirical sketches so long as his
editors and his health permitted.[22] Such a plan would
prove neither difficult nor exhausting; but for whatever
reasons, his ambitions grew and changed in the course
of writing, and there is no evidence that Melville ever
attempted to sell his book that way to either *Harper's* or
Putnam's. Instead, his literary aspirations were to become much higher, especially in the second half of his
book, than he probably imagined they would be when he
began his novel. The nature of those aspirations is to be
found in chapter 44, his interpolated commentary on
original characters.

Chapter 44 offers a glimpse of Melville's germinal relation to his subject and provides clues to the way he
probably went about developing his material, but it also
provides suggestive hints about his final aspirations for
his character. He had found a character "in town" rife
with latent significance that could be developed in his
narrative. This was a compositional method familiar to
him from his recent experience as a short-story writer,
but it was a hazardous one for an extended piece of
fiction. His customary method of development of novels required a fund of personal experiences which might
provide the necessary emotional involvement and rec-
ollected details to sustain him in the protracted telling
of his story. He might amplify and embroider his tale
and supplement his own experience with his reading, as
he had done in earlier romances, but personal experience was the foundation for extended narration. His own
experience in 1840 on a Mississippi riverboat proved too
slender or too insignificant to provide this basis—though
the discarded fragment "The River" suggests that he
might have contemplated this familiar method.[23] In any
event, without an involved narrator and a wealth of re-

membered experiences to give it coherence, Melville's story may well have threatened to disintegrate.

For this reason the title figure played a particularly significant role in the development of Melville's narrative. Not only did the confidence man inspire his subject, but the created character based on him might provide a structural principle as well, one that could connect and give coherence to otherwise discrete and unrelated episodes. The experience of writing *Israel Potter* had taught Melville that a central character could be used in this way, but by the time he came to have his confidence man masquerade as the cosmopolitan, his ambition for the character had transcended its original, narrowly satirical, and conveniently structural function, and he ultimately sought to create a truly original character in the figure of the cosmopolitan.

In the title of chapter 44, Melville playfully and ambiguously suggests that this chapter "will be sure of receiving more or less attention from those readers who do not skip it" (238). Not many critics of the book have skipped this chapter, but perhaps they have not given it the necessary "careful perusal" (a phrase Melville used in an earlier draft of the chapter title).[24] It is, in fact, a chapter about original characters and his own attempt to create one in the figure of the cosmopolitan, though it masquerades as a discursive explanation of why the application of the phrase *quite an original* to the cosmopolitan is ill advised.

"True, we sometimes hear," he wrote, "of an author who, at one creation, produces some two or three score such characters; it may be possible. But they can hardly be original in the sense that Hamlet is, or Don Quixote, or Milton's Satan. That is to say, they are not, in a thorough sense, original at all. They are novel, or singular, or striking, or captivating, or all four at once" (238).[25] That Melville should balk at the suggestion that a novel might contain any number of new or original characters is to his credit. When one recalls the admirably drawn figures that fill the pages of *The Confidence-Man*—Pitch,

the Missouri bachelor; Charlie Noble, the Mississippi
operator; Black Guinea; the Titan; Egbert; and Mark
Winsome—it is evident that Melville could populate
his fiction with memorable characters easily enough.
But apparently he did not believe they possessed anything more than a certain "striking" quality. Nor, finally,
could he claim true originality for even the most interesting character in the book, Frank Goodman, the
cosmopolitan. The supposed purpose of chapter 44 is
to show that that character is undeserving of the descriptive phrase *quite an original.*

Yet the fact that he compared his character to such
original creations as those of Shakespeare, Cervantes,
and Milton testifies to his high ambitions for him. What
may well have begun as the impulse to explore the significance of his character and through him to fashion a
simple strategy for connecting discrete satirical episodes
obviously changed in the course of writing. The subor-
dination of dramatic effects to a prominent central character seems to be what Melville had in mind when he
compared original characters such as Hamlet to a Drummond light, which "rays away from itself" and lights all
that comes within its sphere.

This chapter has obvious reference to Melville's own
created character and his highest aspirations for it. Even
discounting, as the narrator insists we do, for the failure of
Goodman to rival true originals, the achievement is still
impressive. From the moment Frank Goodman makes
his appearance with the words "A penny for your thoughts,
my fine fellow" (130), our attention is focused on a character whose identity and motives are mysterious to us,
yet who is altogether fascinating and complete. This is
not to say that the confidence man in his other manifestations is not "striking" or "singular," but it is in the
cosmopolitan that Melville strove to create a true original. As we shall see, the confidence man in his previous disguises is often derivative and serves in the main
as a satirical vehicle, not as a figure with whom its
creator might easily identify. The cosmopolitan, on the
other hand, often serves as a spokesman for Melville's

own deeply held convictions and at times represents the author's feelings toward his own situation. Moreover, that character is largely the result of the author's attempts to emulate the creators of those original characters he names in chapter 44, each of whom exerted his peculiar influence upon the formation of Frank Goodman.

Melville may have succeeded better than he knew in creating a character that, in all of its disguises, "rays away from itself all around it." As Warner Berthoff has asserted, the final importance of *The Confidence-Man* is the "catholicity of its reach":

> not only that it spans a broad range of occasions and analogous further concerns. With a vividness of emphasis that seems, as we observe it, to surprise life itself, the thrust of imagination in *The Confidence-Man* creates—according to the angle and mass of its local attack—the very scenes it so solidly particularizes.[26]

Which is to say that those very "significances" Melville found in his material had an urgency of interest and breadth of application that he effectively dramatized by the very situation the confidence man himself creates.

There remains, then, the task of identifying the "reach" of this book. The best way to do this, as I have suggested, is through a systematic examination of the title character as he developed in Melville's imagination and provided the occasion for rendering those significances suggested to the author, not simply because Melville's initial interest seems to have been in a real criminal who could be appropriated for the uses of social satire, nor simply because the coherence and structure of the book depended upon his title figure, but primarily because it was on his created character that Melville ultimately wagered the achievement of his book. We shall move then, in the following chapters, through those significances that he found in his material, significances that often mimicked his mood, from the cultural to the philosophical and, finally, to the literary.

George Caleb Bingham, *Pioneer*, 1851.
The St. Louis Art Museum.

Chapter 2

The Man in Town and Other Nineteenth-Century Types

During the summer of 1849, while Melville was in New York City furiously working on *Redburn* and *White-Jacket*, he might well have read the first published account of the original confidence man, entitled "Arrest of the Confidence Man," which appeared in the *New York Herald* on 8 July 1849.[1] The article described the duping of Mr. Thomas McDonald the previous May and the swindler's subsequent arrest in July. A man of "genteel" appearance, after some preliminary conversation, bluntly inquired of McDonald: "Have you confidence in me to trust me with your watch until to-morrow?" McDonald's trust in the stranger, later identified as "Wm. Thompson," resulted in the loss of a one-hundred-ten-dollar watch to the "Confidence Man" and the addition of a new term to the language.

Melville was probably familiar with this first notice of the confidence man, for in his novel he had the cosmopolitan propose, without success, to hold the Missouri bachelor's watch. In chapter 18, after an elaborate debate on the virtues of confidence, the cosmopolitan attempts to strike a bargain with the misanthropic Pitch:

> "My arm, and let's a turn. They are to have dancing on the hurricane-deck to-night. I shall fling them off a Scotch jig, while, to save the pieces, you hold my loose change; and following that, I propose that you, my dear fellow, stack your gun, and throw your bearskins in a sailor's hornpipe—I holding your watch. What do you say?" (135)

If by chance Melville was not acquainted with this particular newspaper article, however, the original confidence man was so popular a figure in the news that

19

summer that the author would have had to make a con-
centrated effort to avoid some contact with the story.
Three days after the first notice of the swindler, the
Herald published a satirical piece entitled "The Confidence Man on a Large Scale."[2] The author of the article
extended the tricks of a petty criminal beyond the realm
of common rascality into the area of high finance. The
original confidence man was detestable, the writer suggested, because he didn't play for high-enough stakes.
America's truly skilled confidence men lived in fabulous apartments in the fashionable part of the city. The
wealth of these well-to-do confidence men, he concluded, was the product of "the same genius in their propri-
etors, which has made the 'Confidence Man' immortal
and a prisoner at 'the Tombs.' His genius has been employed in Wall Street. That's all the difference." This
particular article was very popular and widely reprinted
and would have been available to Melville in one publication or another throughout the summer.[3]

Indeed, the confidence man enjoyed a great deal of
notoriety for the next several months. *The National
Police Gazette* wrote extensively about this figure from
his first appearance in July through October, attempting
to sensationalize his exploits by suggesting that he and
the district attorney were in league. Even Melville's literary friend and publisher, Evert Duyckinck, remarked
upon the criminal in the *Literary World*, though in a more
optimistic vein. In August, Duyckinck reprinted a col-
umn that had first appeared in the *Merchant's Ledger* in
the *Literary World* and supplied an introductory para-
graph that identified the confidence man as a "new species of Jeremy Diddler recently a subject of police finger-
ing, and still later impressed into the service of Burton's
comicalities in Chambers street."[4] Duyckinck further
claimed that the swindler's success on the streets of
New York testified to man's charitable humanity rather
than to his foolish gullibility: "It is not the worst thing
that can be said of a country that it gives birth to a
confidence man."

The piece from the *Merchant's Ledger* had suggested that the man who cannot be swindled is more deserving of our sympathy than the victims of the confidence man: "The man who is *always* on his guard, *always* proof against appeal, who cannot be beguiled into the weakness of pity by *any* story—is far gone, in our opinion, towards being himself a hardened villain." The writer for the *Ledger* also saw the confidence man as representative of respected social types—offering amusing portraits of the "confidence man of politics" and the "confidence man of merchandise"—though he was less anxious to condemn socially established confidence men than was the satirist for the *Herald*.

Melville was certainly familiar with the *Literary World*—he subscribed to it and had written essays for it—and he could have easily read this brief article that summer. And he might have returned to the article when he began writing his book since he probably had saved his back copies of the magazine. Moreover, Duyckinck's allusion to the fact that the confidence man had recently been "impressed into the service of Burton's comicalities" indicates the editor's familiarity with a popular farce produced that summer in William E. Burton's Chambers Street Theatre and suggests another possible source for Melville's acquaintance with the story of the confidence man.

This brief drama, apparently an interlude, was first produced on 23 July 1849, just over two weeks after the arrest of the original confidence man; it was probably the composition of John Brougham, a friend and associate of William Burton.[5] Although no script survives, *The Confidence Man* seems to have been a piece of good fun calculated to win the approval of an audience already familiar with the title character. In fact, the great success of this farce was probably due less to its intrinsic literary merits than to a current public interest in the subject matter. Burton and Brougham were quick to capitalize on a character who had already proved himself interesting to the public. More than that, however, the rapid production and easy success of *The Confidence Man* indicate how readily the exploits of William Thompson might be translated into comic and dramatic form. If Melville did not mark how susceptible the original confidence man was to "literary use" in the summer of 1849, there were others who did, and they profited by that use.[6]

Melville was too busy writing *White-Jacket* that summer, and too busy making publication arrangements for the book in England that fall, to give much thought to a literary project based on the original confidence man. He did, however, acquire the *Life and Remarkable Adventures of Israel R. Potter* (1824) while he was in London and apparently planned to put the book to literary use, for he made notes for a story about this Revolutionary patriot.[7] Although Melville was looking for literary material, and though he was probably familiar with the original confidence man, whatever interest he may have taken at the time in the newspaper accounts of William Thompson or the farce produced on Chambers Street probably was not of a literary nature, for there is no evidence that he then planned to write a story about a confidence man; it would require a second acquaintance with this criminal to jar his memory. A second acquaintance was forthcoming, for the original confidence man reemerged closer to home, in Albany in April 1855.

On 28 April 1855, the *Albany Evening Journal* published a brief account of the original confidence man's most recent adventure:

The Original Confidence Man in Town— A Short Chapter on Misplaced Confidence

He called into a jewelry store on Broadway and said to the proprietor: "How do you do, Mr. Myers?" Receiving no reply, he added "Don't you know me?" to which Mr. M. replied that he did not. "My name is Samuel Willis. You are mistaken, for I have met you three or four times." He then said he had something of a private nature to communicate to Mr. Myers and that he wished to see him alone. The two men walked to the end of the counter, when Willis said to

Myers, "I guess you are a Mason,"—to which Myers replied
that he was—when Willis asked him if he would not give a
brother a shilling if he needed it. By some shrewd management, Myers was induced to give him six or seven dollars.[8]

Melville was clearly acquainted with this newspaper
article, also reprinted in the *Springfield Republican* on
4 May, for he had his fictional confidence man use iden-
tical tactics in his novel. In chapter 4, "Renewal of Old
Acquaintance," John Ringman, the man with the weed,
"renews" his acquaintance with Mr. Roberts:

"How do you do, Mr. Roberts?"
"Eh?"
"Don't you know me?"
"No, certainly." (18)

Ringman proceeds to gain the merchant's confidence by
inventing incidents in the supposed history of their acquaintance and by delivering a lecture on the inconstancy
of one's memory, especially when one has received an
accidental blow to the head. In addition, the confidence
man calls Mr. Roberts to one side and overcomes the
merchant's remaining suspicions by claiming to be a
fellow member of the Masons:

"If I remember, you are a mason, Mr. Roberts?"
"Yes, yes."
Averting himself a moment, as to recover from a return of
agitation, the stranger grasped the other's hand; "and would
you not loan a brother a shilling if he needed it?" (21)

Both the *Albany Evening Journal* and the *Springfield
Republican* were available to a man living in nearby
Pittsfield, Massachusetts. If Melville read the item in
the *Evening Journal*, he no doubt would have read as
well a separate piece not reprinted in the Springfield
paper entitled "Brief History of the Confidence Man."
This article identified "Samuel Willis" as the original
confidence man arrested in New York City six years
before, and it furnished a history of the confidence man's
prior criminal activities. Samuel Willis, alias "William
Thompson," was still sufficiently newsworthy for the

New York Daily Tribune and the *New York Daily Times*
to reprint a second article about the confidence man
published by the *Evening Journal* on 5 May 1855. This
second article told of a visit by a New York City police-
man who confirmed that Samuel Willis was "No. 1, the
Original Confidence Man."[9]

The original confidence man seems to have retained a
certain reputation that distinguished him from other
confidence-man types, such as forgers, gamblers, counterfeiters, and the like, who thrived in nineteenth-century
America. Apparently, what made this criminal fascinating and set him apart from other contemporary rogues
was not the magnitude of his swindles, nor a malicious
and dangerous character, but the originality of his tactics. Many newspaper accounts of the confidence man
used the words *original, new,* or *genius* to describe him,
but the word *original* was used most often and used in
a variety of ways for a variety of purposes. By designat-
ing Thompson (or "Willis," or any of the other aliases
he employed) the "original" confidence man, a newspaper
writer meant to distinguish him from all other criminals
who preyed upon the sympathies of the unwary. And it
was generally recognized that Thompson's blunt appeal
for confidence gave birth to the term *confidence man.*

In a larger cultural context, the original confidence
man suggested a multitude of social and economic com-
parisons. The satirist for the *Herald* used the story of
the confidence man to expose the "true" confidence
men in America, the men of Wall Street. *The National
Police Gazette,* in attempting to link the confidence
man with the district attorney, sought to expose the
fraud and corruption of City Hall. And the reporter for
the *Merchant's Ledger* identified still other types of confidence men: the "young confidence man of politics"
and "the confidence man of merchandise." Even for men
whose imaginations were perhaps not so alert to "significances" as was Melville's, the original confidence man
was rich in "suggestiveness," and the ability of this character to suggest other American types was an important

part of his originality. For Melville's part, it seems clear that the newspaper items that dealt with the original confidence man aroused a desire to put the original character to "literary use." Melville had found his "original" character "in town," and that character would provide the writer with an idea and the title for his book.

There was very little factual information about the confidence man published by newspapers and periodicals. Nevertheless, Melville does include in his novel nearly all the "facts" known about the original confidence man; and, as with the Agatha letter, he moves quite easily from the fact to its implication. In chapter 4, the author used the dialogue between Samuel Willis and Mr. Myers as it was presented in the *Albany Evening Journal* almost verbatim. The episode also suggested to Melville an opportunity for his character to lecture on the inconstancy of man's "faithless" memory and the "ductile" quality of the human mind. Whatever "genius" the original confidence man may have possessed, it is unlikely that it was for such discourse. Rather, the actual episode possessed for Melville a certain "significance" and gave his own confidence man the opportunity to "philosophize" a bit.

If Melville's own memory was less "faithless" than Mr. Roberts's, he may have recalled that the first reports of the capture of the original confidence man emphasized the criminal's blunt appeal for confidence. The *Herald* article that first noticed the confidence man quoted his entreaty to Mr. McDonald as "Have you confidence in me to trust me with your watch until to-morrow?"; and the satirical piece that appeared in the *Herald* three days later reported that the confidence man inquired of his victim, "Are you really disposed to put any confidence in me?" Several times in the novel Melville's confidence man makes a similar appeal. In chapter 5, the man with the weed demands of the college sophomore whether he might "by way of experiment, simply have confidence in *me?*" (27). In chapter 8, the man in gray addresses a similar question to a "charitable lady": "Could you put confidence in *me* for instance?" (44). In chapter 15, after the man with the traveling cap has given the parched miser a drink of water, he asks, as repayment for this charitable action, that the old man give him his confidence and a hundred dollars. And, in chapter 42, the cosmopolitan inquires of the barber, "As a supposition—you would have confidence in me, wouldn't you?" (227).

Another apparent "fact" about the original confidence man was that he was some sort of genius, but a genius who was willing to play for very small stakes. Indeed, the *Herald* satire was based upon the obvious discrepancy between a man of intelligence and nerve who was content to swindle his victims out of a few dollars and his wealthier counterparts, the confidence men of Wall Street. Melville, too, alludes to the genius of his confidence man indirectly when he remarks that the poster offering a reward for the capture of a "mysterious impostor" describes "quite an original genius in his vocation, as would appear, though wherein his originality consisted was not clearly given" (3). Melville's confidence man also plays for small stakes quite often. Black Guinea shuffles about the deck of the *Fidèle* for odd coins tossed his way. The herb doctor sells his medicine for a half-dollar a vial. The P.I.O. man, after lengthy debate, manages to pry a mere three dollars from the pocket of Pitch, the Missouri bachelor. And the cosmopolitan takes great pains to diddle the barber out of the price of a shave.

However, despite the fact that the real confidence man seemed content to employ his genius for small rewards, Melville may have anticipated objections to the realism of a fictional character who did so. In chapter 33, the narrator refers to those readers of fiction who "look not only for more entertainment, but, at bottom, even for more reality, than real life itself can show" (183). At any rate, there is some speculation in the novel about the motives of Black Guinea.

In chapter 6, the man in gray and the young clergyman (who had earlier defended the character of Black Guinea) debate with the one-legged man about the true nature of the Negro cripple. The man in gray attempts to refute the claim that Black Guinea is a fraud by arguing that the cripple's rewards were hardly worth his efforts:

> "I think that without personal proof I can convince you of your mistake. For I put it to you, is it reasonable to suppose that a man with brains, sufficient to act such a part as you say, would take all that trouble, and run all that hazard, for the mere sake of those few paltry coppers, which, I hear, was all he got for his pains, if pains they were?"
>
> "That puts the case irrefutably," said the young clergyman, with a challenging glance towards the one-legged man.
>
> "You two green-horns! Money, you think, is the sole motive to pains and hazard, deception and deviltry, in this world. How much money did the devil make by gulling Eve?" (32)

Some have suggested that the one-legged man's rebuke testifies to the devilish nature of Melville's confidence man. However, the real criminal was perfectly willing to risk pains and hazard for a "few paltry coppers." In the same way that he had insisted that the postbox should be included in the Agatha story, Melville may have felt the compulsion to account for a puzzling fact about the original confidence man. And the "author of 'Typee' and 'Omoo' " might well have sympathized with a man who had been accused, albeit satirically, of wasting his genius on financially unprofitable schemes, since reviewers had often accused Melville of wasting his talents in the production of *Mardi*, *Moby-Dick*, and especially *Pierre*.[10] Moreover, there is an element of gamesmanship involved in the schemes of the fictional confidence man; rather than a malicious felon, Melville seems to have seen this character as a playful rogue and mischiefmaker.

There are, of course, more general characteristics that the original confidence man must have possessed and that Melville could have easily deduced without the aid of newspaper or magazine articles. The original confidence man, in order to approach, much less swindle, any man wealthy enough to carry a one-hundred-ten-dollar watch on his person, must himself have seemed a respectable gentleman. The first newspaper notice of the confidence man had pointed out that the criminal had a certain "genteel appearance," and the *Herald* satire informed its readers that part of the original confidence man's "financial genius" was his "powers of moral suasion" and his "easy *nonchalance.*" Certainly, Melville's confidence man displays all of these characteristics in several of his roles.

Some of the presumed masquerades of Melville's confidence man, however, are not particularly "genteel." The mute is dressed in a suit of cream colors, which, though it is neither "soiled nor slovenly," has a certain "tossed" look about it (6). Black Guinea, of course, is dressed in tatters, and the herb doctor is somewhat shabby in appearance. The representative of the Philosophical Intelligence Office assumes "as genteel an attitude as the irritating set of his pinched five-dollar suit would permit" (120). The man with the weed and the man in gray, on the other hand, appear to be a good deal more acceptable in appearance; the narrator describes them as belonging to that group of "less unrefined children of misfortune" (28). And the man with the traveling cap is apparently attired appropriately for the president of the Black Rapids Coal Company. But it is the cosmopolitan who truly sparkles in appearance; he is dressed as a "king of traveled good-fellows," though the Missouri bachelor believes the cosmopolitan's genteel appearance indicates "fine feathers on foul meat" (131). Indeed, the cosmopolitan, dressed in a coat of "various hues," maroon slippers, and a purple smoking cap, seems a caricature of refinement.

In the "powers of moral suasion" the cosmopolitan also excels, though ironically his attempts to gull the passengers are far less successful than his earlier adventures in other roles. The cosmopolitan has a "sweet" voice (130) and the "power of persuasive fascination"

(234). Indeed, the barber would remember the cosmopolitan as "the man-charmer" (237). But in other roles the confidence man is also quite persuasive. The man with the weed confesses his reasons for mourning to Mr. Roberts in a tale "involving calamities against which no integrity, no forethought, no energy, no genius, no piety, could guard" (21). The man in gray possesses equal powers: "A not unsilvery tongue, too, was his, with gestures that were a Pentecost of added ones, and persuasiveness before which granite hearts might crumble into gravel" (42). The man with the traveling cap persuades a suspicious miser to invest a hundred dollars in his coal company; and the herb doctor talks the same miser into purchasing a vial of his "Omni-Balsamic Reinvigorator." In varying degrees the confidence man, in all his roles, is exceptionally persuasive.

Perhaps the most "nonchalant" character aboard the *Fidèle* is the herb doctor. He faces the suffering Titan in chapter 17 with remarkable self-possession. The giant challenges the doctor's claims for the "Samaritan Pain Dissuader" in an obviously vindictive spirit and finally strikes the herb doctor across the face. Throughout the interview, however, the doctor seems in "no way abashed," and as the anger rises in the Titan, the confidence man addresses him in "a tone more assured than before." Even after he has suffered the blow from the Titan, the herb doctor recovers quickly and has the presence of mind to apply his own medicine to the bruise in plain view of his would-be customers. In chapter 21, the herb doctor faces the potentially dangerous Pitch, who is continually snapping his rifle as a warning to beware, and the doctor replies to each charge brought against him "with manly intrepidity forbearing each unmanly thrust" (113).

The precise degree to which Melville put his knowledge of the original confidence man to literary use remains a matter of speculation. The evidence shows, however, that he used material from the newspaper accounts of both 1849 and 1855 and that he began with the latter in chapter 4 when John Ringman, like "Samuel Willis," "renews" his supposed acquaintance with an old friend and identifies himself as a fellow Mason. The frequency with which Melville's deceiver pleads for "confidence" from his intended victim indicates that the original character remained in the author's mind during the episodes that followed, and he may have derived the idea of expanding the range of the confidence man's activities from suggestions contained in various newspaper stories in 1849 dealing with the activities of "William Thompson." In chapter 24, however, when Frank Goodman tries to relieve Pitch of his watch, Melville had clearly gone back to the original story; and the piece Duyckinck reprinted in the *Literary World* apparently supplied him with the idea of changing the direction of his satire by using his "Jeremy Diddler" to attack those who were "*always* on . . . guard, *always* proof against appeal" and "who cannot be beguiled into the weakness of pity by *any* story."[11]

However ambiguous some of the connections may be, it is evident that Melville took for the central character of his book a real person who had been picked up "in town" in 1849 and again in 1855 and that he took his title from the descriptive phrase that had been applied to that swindler and that was a new term in the language. It is also evident that Melville found the story of the confidence man, as he had found the story of Agatha Robertson, "instinct with significance"—a "skeleton of reality" that could be "built about" with realistic and symbolic associations until it achieved the "fulness" of a novel. The most realistic of these associations were the many types of fraudulent schemes and as many types of rogues and impostors that flourished in nineteenth-century America and often came together on a Mississippi riverboat of the sort he adopted as the setting for his story.

Melville's treatment of knaves and rogues in *The Confidence-Man* is comprehensive. To the journalists who had written about the original confidence man, he was an emblem for the greater social and moral malaise existing in nineteenth-century America; he was a walking, talking metaphor for types of swindlers, some socially respectable and some not, who preyed upon the faith of the unwary. And certainly Melville, no less than these journalists, recognized the metaphoric possibilities of the original confidence man. While the confidence man might have provided an occasion for a discussion of other types of confidence men and confidence games, he served as little more than a focal point for an examination of fraud and deception on a larger scale. There were many other artists of deception who walked the streets of New York or worked the crowds aboard Mississippi riverboats, and in his novel Melville makes use of or alludes to nearly every other type of contemporary scheme or swindler on record. Moreover, he satirically exposes other kinds of confidence games or confidence men not generally believed to be disreputable. While the actions of a single confidence man may have provided the initial inspiration for his novel, there were other types of confidence men or confidence games that the author put to literary use.

Johannes Bergmann has thoroughly researched the criminal element in American society prior to 1857 in his dissertation and has provided a geographically organized rogues' gallery.[12] New England fraudulent operators included church impostors, Yankee peddlers, and rogues whose autobiographies or biographies were published in the first part of the nineteenth century. The Southwestern species of confidence man includes "wolves," outright murderers and thieves such as Samuel Meason, the Harpe brothers, and John Murrell, all of whom Melville alludes to in the opening chapter of his novel; "clowns," literary characters such as J. J. Hooper's "Simon Suggs," Joseph Baldwin's "Ovid Bolus," and others; and "gamblers." New York City gave rise to certain "urban criminals": impostors and forgers; fraudulent businessmen who were particularly fond of the hoax (Bergmann cites P.

T. Barnum as the prime example of this sort of rascal);
and "professors of appropriation," men who celebrated
humbug and played upon the gullibility of the public
(James Gordon Bennett, editor of the *New York Herald*,
is the chief example of this type of huckster).

Bergmann's dissertation is an exhaustive treatment
of confidence men and their prototypes operating in
America prior to the publication of *The Confidence-Man*
and offers a multitude of possible sources of material for
Melville's novel in addition to the original confidence
man. Bergmann identifies many of the tactics and devices used by shysters—including the deaf-and-dumb
act, which was used more than once, incidentally, by
the Yankee peddler William Avery Rockefeller, father of
John D. Rockefeller.[13] And he argues quite persuasively
against Daniel Hoffman's assertion that Melville patterned his confidence man after the typical Yankee peddler. However, except for the fascinating information
included about the original confidence man, the most
valuable aspect of Bergmann's study is that it establishes
the general climate of fraud and deception present before and during the period in which Melville wrote *The
Confidence-Man* by presenting a variety of intriguing
criminals with a large inventory of ingenious confidence
games, which might well have interested Melville and
the public at large.

Melville fully exploited this criminal climate, often
using criminal types and criminal techniques to lend an
air of authenticity to his treatment of the subject, and
often using the tactics of confidence men to expose the
parallel tactics of men not usually thought of as confidence men. As social satire, *The Confidence-Man* appears to have a double aim: first, to satirize a society
that allows confidence men to flourish at its expense,
and, second, to satirize those individuals within it who
were too skeptical or cold-blooded to be victimized. Though
the literary use Melville makes of other types of confidence men and confidence games is frequently secondary to the central character's blunt appeal for confidence,

it is an important aspect of the novel, for *The Confidence-Man* at least touches upon a great many of the contemporary types of swindles aimed at an unsuspecting or foolish public.

Both James Fenimore Cooper in *Home as Found* (1838) and Dickens in *Martin Chuzzlewit* (1843) had dealt with certain types of land fraud in the United States, including the sale of towns not yet built. Melville makes casual use of the same theme when he has the president of the Black Rapids Coal Company offer the college sophomore a chance to invest in "New Jerusalem." Even the naive sophomore demonstrates some familiarity with this type of swindle, for he immediately asks whether the buildings are in fact "standing" and whether any of the sites available for purchase are not actually "water-lots" (50).

The author also briefly alludes to the practice of counterfeiting in America when, in the final chapter, he has a beggar boy, who peddles door locks and money belts, give an old man a "Counterfeit Detector" as a free bonus for his purchase of more than seventy-five cents worth of merchandise.[14] The "Counterfeit Detector" is yet another item that belongs in the same category of protection devices as the money belt, the door lock, and even the life-preserver stool upon which the old man sits. The appeal of these items lies less in the confidence of the customer in the product or the salesman than in the distrust one has for his fellowman and the fears one has about natural catastrophes. In this scene, as in others, the action of the characters comments on the subject under discussion. Here, the old man's purchase of devices to protect him from his fellowman and the discovery of the life preserver to protect him from acts of Providence interrupt a discussion of the virtues of trust.

Melville also demonstrates his knowledge of other types of fraudulent products that did appeal to the confidence of their purchasers. There were, of course, miracle cures and contraptions promising quick relief from pain and suffering. The medicines that the herb doctor

sells to the passengers of the *Fidèle* are ironically named
the "Omni-Balsamic Reinvigorator" and the "Samaritan Pain Dissuader." And the man in gray claims to have
invented the "Protean easy-chair," which will give com-
fort to the "most restless body" and perhaps soothe "the
most tormented conscience" (38).[15] The herb doctor's
natural curatives may be, as Elizabeth Foster has suggested, Melville's satirical version of the once popular
"Dr. Brandreth's Pills," which were advertised as "purely
vegetable" cure-alls.[16] And, as Ms. Foster also explains,
William Raglan, a Philadelphia manufacturer, exhibited
reclining chairs at the Crystal Palace in 1851; these chairs
may have inspired Melville's "Protean easy-chair."[17]

References to products such as herb medicines and
money belts, easy chairs and counterfeit detectors, are
scattered throughout *The Confidence-Man*, and as concrete details they lend a certain authenticity to the narrative and poke fun at those who, either out of desire or
fear, provide a market for such products. But Melville
also found that another literary use might be made of
the schemes of confidence men as well. The author of
the *Herald* satire had made a telling comparison between
an actual confidence man and the confidence men of
Wall Street. Melville, too, was quick to perceive that
swindlers' techniques, which by their association with
criminal, antisocial activities would naturally be judged
as undesirable, might be made to comment on socially
acceptable activities and respected social types. With
far greater subtlety than the *Herald* satirist, Melville
was able to use his knowledge of criminal activities for
his own purposes.

In a Shakespearean manner, Melville often has the
scene of action or the actions of the characters themselves either complement or contradict the dialogue of
the characters. In this way, the author frequently injects
an added dimension of humor or suggests an ironic contrast to the topic under discussion; without disturbing
the flow of conversation, Melville frequently manipu-
lates the background or action as a kind of stylistic coun-

terpoint to the already ambiguous surfaces of the characters' dialogue.

In chapter 21, the herb doctor, accompanied by his
most recent customer, the sick miser, confronts the skeptical Pitch. Pitch claims to have confidence in neither
nature nor man, a point of view that understandably
disturbs the miser, who has just placed his confidence in
the herb doctor and the natural medicines he sells. The
herb doctor, of course, undertakes to defend both nature
and man against Pitch's criticism. Throughout the debate, however, the miser's reliance on the herb doctor
proves to be an increasing discomfort. The herb doctor
invites the miser to lean against him rather than the
boat's railing, and "the two stood together; the old miser
leaning against the herb-doctor with something of that
air of trustful fraternity with which, when standing, the
less strong of the Siamese twins habitually leans against
the other" (108). That "trustful fraternity" begins to
break down, however, as the herb doctor feels the weight
of the miser's trust. From time to time, the herb doctor
interrupts his debate with the Missouri bachelor to advise the miser to support part of the weight himself,
complaining to the ailing passenger, "you lean rather
hard." Finally, making the irony of the situation explicit, the Missouri bachelor advises the miser to "go lay
down in your grave, old man, if you can't stand of yourself. It's a hard world for a leaner" (111). Not only do
these intrusions nullify the herb doctor's defense of unqualified confidence in man and nature, but they also
expose the herb doctor as a hypocrite and the miser
as a pathetic dupe whose weakness is moral as well as
physical.

Another example of this stylistic device is to be found
in chapters 42 and 43, where the cosmopolitan encounters the barber, William Cream. In this episode both
characters alternately apply their own special brand of
"lather" to the other. Throughout their interview, which is
interlarded with puns, among them the punning use of the
words *smooth* and *lather*, the cosmopolitan tries to smooth

talk the barber into removing his sign of No Trust. But
the barber cannot shave his customer unless the cosmopolitan refrains from his smooth talk, and the cosmopolitan cannot *shave* the barber unless he is allowed
to apply his own verbal lather. In the end, however, both
shaves are completed. The cosmopolitan not only persuades the barber to remove his sign, but he also avoids
paying for the shave.

In yet another episode Melville couples this satirical
device with his knowledge of gamblers and gambling in
order to expose financial investment as but another form
of gambling. Although Melville's confidence man never
masquerades as a gambler, there is a scene in which the
president of the Black Rapids Coal Company and the
merchant comment on a game of cards in progress across
the room. In his handling of this episode, the author
subtly suggests that gambling and investing are related
activities.

In chapter 10 of *The Confidence-Man*, the man in the
traveling cap casually sits beside the merchant, Mr. Roberts, and places the transfer book for the coal company
in plain view between them. Across the cabin, two "un-
polished youths" are opposed in a game of whist to two
middle-aged men dressed in "professional black." The
merchant confesses that he is not familiar with "such
gentry" except through reading about them and asks the
man in the traveling cap if those are not "sharpers" opposed to the youths. The president of the coal company
rebukes his companion for his "fault finding spirit" and
lack of confidence. Ironically, while the confidence man
is defending the sharps, he is at the same time using the
techniques of a professional gambler to lure the merchant into investing in his coal company. And the merchant, supposedly unfamiliar with gamblers and gambling, betrays his own gambling instincts.

The methods of the professional gambler are artfully
employed by the confidence man. He suckers the merchant into investing in his coal company by masquerad-
ing as someone too refined to be suspected for a cheat;

and when the merchant pleads for a chance to invest, the confidence man feigns disinterest. Moreover, Mr. Roberts, the merchant, had been "set up" prior to his meeting with this confidence man. Black Guinea had mentioned a "ge'mman wid a big book" along with other "honest" gentlemen (13); and later the man with the weed had informed the merchant, as a favor for the loan received from him, that there might be an opportunity to invest in the Black Rapids Coal Company, assuring him that a small investment would reap a handsome profit. All of these techniques were the stock-in-trade of the professional gambler, though similar schemes might have been used by other types of swindlers.[18] Since the merchant and the man with the traveling cap first enter into a conversation on the gamblers across the way, the episode clearly invites a comparison between gambling and investment. And the fact that the confidence man, posing as a businessman, uses tactics that might equally be employed by a professional gambler amply demonstrates the irony and subtlety with which Melville suggests the analogy.

Allusions to a multitude of swindlers and schemes may be found in *The Confidence-Man.* The author casually alludes to the existence of bandits and pickpockets, gamblers and counterfeiters. He uses known tactics of unscrupulous characters, such as the popular deaf-and-dumb act or a plan for "international improvement." And he has Black Guinea act the part of a painted decoy who, in his humble way, recommends to the crowd those "good, kind, honest ge'mmen" (13) aboard the *Fidèle,* gentlemen who, as we shall see, are usually the same man in disguise. In fact, of all the deceptive tactics used by confidence men, Melville makes the most ingenious and liberal use of this particular ploy. The man with the weed and the man in gray attest to Guinea's honesty. The man with the weed informs the college sophomore and the merchant that the president of the Black Rapids Coal Company is aboard the boat. The man with the traveling cap, after swindling him himself, advises the miser to let the herb doctor cure him. And after the herb doctor learns of Pitch's need for a boy helper, the P.I.O. man appears, claiming to be able to supply the Missourian with a truly reliable boy.

Moreover, in at least one episode, Melville seems to draw upon the tradition of American rogue literature. As Bergmann has shown, one of the most popular elements in literature dealing with the American criminal, whether it be autobiography, exposé, or fiction, is the unknowing confrontation of one confidence man with another. Such confrontations were related in many contemporary exposés of gambling, counterfeiting, deceptive business practices, and the like. And in fiction, the title character in J. J. Hooper's *The Adventures of Simon Suggs* (1845), who had once cheated his father in a card game, feels compelled to match his skill with the "Tigers," the polished professional gamblers. But perhaps the most widely known formulation of the encounter of two or more unscrupulous characters in literature is the "horse swap," which Longstreet treated in *Georgia Scenes* as early as 1835 and which Faulkner included in *The Hamlet*. It is somewhat surprising, therefore, that many modern readers of *The Confidence-Man* should be puzzled by the chapters in which one rogue confronts another.

Actually such encounters occur at least four times in the novel. The herb doctor meets with a "soldier of fortune" in chapters 18 and 19. This man, who poses as a wounded soldier in order to receive alms from sympathetic passengers, is actually a veteran of the Tombs in New York.[19] Similarly, the encounter between the cosmopolitan and the boat's barber, as we shall see in the last chapter, is a meeting of confidence men, though no one has demonstrated this before. And in the final chapter of *The Confidence-Man*, the cosmopolitan's conversation with a kind, faithful old man is interrupted by the intrusion of a boy peddler who caters to the distrust of the riverboat passengers. But the most controversial encounter is that of Frank Goodman with Charlie Noble.

From Charlie Noble's appearance in chapter 25 until his exit in chapter 36, these two confidence men attempt to dupe each other. Charlie tries to make the cosmopolitan vulnerable to his own confidence game by liberally filling his would-be victim's glass with wine, a beverage Charlie himself only pretends to drink, and engaging in "genial" conversation with his "boon companion." However, the cosmopolitan spoils the designs of the operator by making the first appeal for a friendly loan, and Charlie, after recovering from his amazement, soon takes his leave.

The entire episode is handled in a humorous way that is perfectly consistent with the comic mode that had been established prior to the publication of *The Confidence-Man* in 1857. Owing to the equally questionable characters of the two men, the reader may feel that either deserves whatever deception and trickery might be practiced upon him; thus the reader may suspend moral judgment of the situation and delight in the ironic comedy involved. Rather than introducing some radical discrepancy into his narrative, Melville was working within a literary tradition, brief though it may have been, when he had the confidence man expose Charlie Noble as a fraud and a cheat.[20] Moreover, it may have occurred to the author that the cosmopolitan could be used to expose other types of confidence men not generally associated with the criminal fraternity.

Not much has been made of the striking parallels between the cosmopolitan's encounter with Charlie Noble, the Mississippi operator, and his encounter with Mark Winsome and Egbert, characters who respectively embody the theoretical and practical aspects of a transcendental philosophy. However, the parallels do exist, and it seems to have been Melville's intention to demonstrate by juxtaposition that Winsome and Egbert are as surely deceptive as Charlie Noble.

Watson Branch has pointed out some of the parallels between these two episodes.[21] Branch observes that an identification between Charlie and Egbert and Winsome is suggested by the fact that Winsome sits in the "still warm" seat that Charlie had occupied earlier, so that perhaps the "genial warmth" and "genial hospitality" of its former occupant might pass from the seat into Winsome. Also, there is an implied identification of Egbert with Charlie in demonstrating the principles of Mark Winsome's philosophy. Charlie and the cosmopolitan had pretended to be "boon companions"; Egbert, assuming the role of Charlie, becomes the cosmopolitan's "hypothetical friend."[22] Branch also notes that just as Charlie had criticized the character of Pitch, so too does Winsome criticize the character of Charlie. After the cosmopolitan has left the Missouri bachelor to his sulk, he is approached by Noble, who immediately calls into question the nature of the backwoodsman: "Rather entertaining old 'coon, if he wasn't so deuced analytical. Reminded me somehow of what I've heard about Colonel John Moredock, of Illinois, only your friend ain't quite so good a fellow at bottom, I should think" (139). In similar fashion, Winsome accosts the cosmopolitan, after Charlie Noble has departed, and suggests that Noble is, in fact, a "Mississippi operator." In both instances, however, the cosmopolitan defends the character of his previous acquaintance against the criticisms of his new companion.

And, as Branch also points out, both Charlie and Egbert relate certain stories, but stories for which neither raconteur claims responsibility. Charlie tells the story of Colonel Moredock, Indian hater, as it was told to him by Judge James Hall, but reminds the cosmopolitan at the conclusion of the tale that it is "not my story, mind, or my thoughts, but another's" (155). And Egbert tells the story of "China Aster" with equal equivocation:

> "I will tell you about China Aster. I wish I could do so in my own words, but unhappily the original story-teller here has so tyrannized over me, that it is quite impossible for me to repeat his incidents without sliding into his style. I fore-

warn you of this, that you may not think me so maudlin as, in some parts, the story would seem to make its narrator." (207)

In addition to these parallels mentioned by Branch, there are still other parallel elements in these two episodes. While these elements may say something about the composition and structure of *The Confidence-Man*, which is Branch's contention, they also reveal much about the ingenuity and subtlety of Melville's tactics of satire. Despite the criticism delivered by Charlie against Pitch and by Winsome against Charlie, the cosmopolitan, true to his nature, immediately warms to the possibility of a new companion. When Charlie invites the cosmopolitan to share a bottle of wine with him, the confidence man is at first reluctant but finally agrees. However, it so happens that the cosmopolitan drinks most of the bottle, while Charlie takes scarcely a thimbleful. Nevertheless, Charlie pretends to love it: "Good wine, good wine; is it not the peculiar bond of good feeling?" (161). Similarly, when the cosmopolitan invites Mark Winsome to share the remaining wine, the mystic confesses his love for the beverage, but declines on the grounds that this love impels him to keep it in the "lasting condition of an untried abstraction" (192). Instead, Winsome, as "coldly radiant as a prism," prefers to drink ice water.

Also, in both episodes, a person of pitiable circumstances is observed by the cosmopolitan and his newfound friend. Charlie Noble bursts into a fit of uncontrollable laughter at the site of a "pale pauper boy" (163), and Winsome coldly ignores a "haggard, inspired looking man" selling some "rhapsodical tract."[23] Although the cosmopolitan courteously purchases a copy, Winsome sits "more like a cold prism than ever, while an expression of keen Yankee cuteness, now replacing his former mystical one, lent added icicles to his aspect" (195). Finally, in both episodes, the cosmopolitan's new acquaintance tells a story designed to prove a certain point; and in both instances the cosmopolitan either denies or mistakes their meaning. Frank Goodman denies that the protagonist of Charlie Noble's story, Colonel Moredock, bears any resemblance to his friend Pitch; in fact he claims to doubt that Moredock ever existed. And Egbert, Winsome's practical disciple, tells the story of China Aster in order to convince Goodman of "the folly, on both sides, of a friend's helping a friend" (221). The cosmopolitan, however, sees the story as an attempt to destroy his confidence in his fellowman. Whether or not Mark Winsome and Egbert are identifiable as actual persons, they are objects of satire, and Melville is certainly satirizing transcendentalist types.[24] Moreover, he is inviting the reader to conclude that these men are confidence men.

Charlie Noble, despite his generous opinions about good fellowship and humor, Noah's press and Shakespeare, soon betrays himself as one whose nature is cold and unfeeling. He, like Mark Winsome, prefers to keep his eye on the "main chance" (198). Thus, like the transcendentalists, he prefers not to cloud his mind with wine. The cosmopolitan, though he denies its wisdom, recalls the advice of an "irreligious Parisian wit" about "gamblers and all sorts of subtle tricksters sticking to cold water, the better to keep a cool head for business" (164). Certainly, by disdaining wine, Charlie Noble and Mark Winsome reveal similar motives.

Mark Winsome informs the cosmopolitan that Charlie Noble is a "Mississippi operator," "an equivocal character" (196), and with good reason; Charlie Noble is no more "noble" than Mark Winsome is "winsome." Noble's convictions are governed by the winds of chance; he adjusts his attitudes according to those of his prospective victims. However, what is equivocation in the Mississippi operator is inconsistency in the transcendental philosopher. As Mark Winsome freely admits, "I seldom care to be consistent. In a philosophical view, consistency is a certain level at all times, maintained in all the thoughts of one's mind. But, since nature is nearly all hill and dale, how can one keep naturally advancing in knowledge without submitting to the natural inequalities in the progress?" (193). Winsome stalks knowledge in the same way that a Mississippi operator stalks his victim: he makes his advances by artful submission. Moreover, Mark Winsome and Egbert seem as unwittingly hypocritical as Charlie Noble is deliberately so. Winsome claims to love "lucidity" above all things, yet his philosophical tenets are incapable of expression in other than unknown Greek and Egyptian phrases. And Egbert's "practical" application of his master's teachings proves practical only insofar as it resists any application.

In the chapter entitled "Hypothetical Friends," Egbert agrees to play the part of Charlie Noble, and Goodman applies to his friend for a loan. Throughout, Goodman's appeals for charity are artfully deflected by Egbert by means of a humorous brand of transcendental logic chopping:

> "For though I am not of the sour mind of Solomon, that, in the hour of need, a stranger is better than a brother; yet, I entirely agree with my sublime master, who, in his Essay on Friendship, says so nobly, that if he wants a terrestrial convenience, not to his friend celestial (or friend social and intellectual) would he go; no: for his terrestrial convenience, to his friend terrestrial (or humbler business-friend) he goes. Very lucidly he adds the reason: Because, for the superior nature, which on no account can ever descend to do good, to be annoyed with requests to do it, when the inferior one, which by no instruction can ever rise above that capacity, stands always inclined to it—this is unsuitable." (204)

By the end of their interview in chapter 41, Egbert has proved to the cosmopolitan that Winsome's philosophy of friendship is equivalent to the transcendalist's love of wine; one's love of man, like his love of wine, is best preserved as an "untried abstraction."

The episodes involving Charlie Noble and Mark Winsome and Egbert evidence a rather protracted use of the

same satirical device Melville used in his treatment of
the man in the traveling cap and the merchant: juxtaposition of a recognized form of swindle and deception
with a form not generally perceived as swindle or deception at all. In the same way that Melville had suggested
that gambling and investment are related activities by
hinting at the similar impulses involved and tactics used,
so does he suggest that the character of a Mississippi
operator resembles the character of a transcendentalist
thinker—equivocal, selfish, and unfeeling.

In his exposure of Mark Winsome and Egbert, Melville seems to side with the author of the article reprinted
in the *Literary World:* the man who is *"always* on his
guard, *always* proof against appeal" is himself a "hardened villain."[25] And of the two confidence-man types,
Melville appears to have less sympathy for the cold transcendentalist. At the conclusion of their interview, the
cosmopolitan is so repulsed by Winsome's philosophy
that he prefers to give rather than receive a charitable
contribution: "Pray, leave me, and with you take the
last dregs of your inhuman philosophy. And here, take
this shilling, and at the first wood-landing buy yourself
a few chips to warm the frozen natures of you and your
philosopher by" (223).

Despite the lengthy treatment of Winsome and Egbert and the pointed satirical thrusts at their transcendental philosophy, *The Confidence-Man* is not merely a
"great transcendental satire," as Carl Van Vechten would
have had us believe.[26] As a careful reading of the novel
soon discloses, *The Confidence-Man* satirizes a much
larger spectrum of human beliefs and activities, from
commerce to religion, from hypocrisy to human gullibility. The cosmopolitan's exposure of the heartless transcendentalists is but another band in this spectrum.

Though the scope of considerations of *The Confidence-Man* is wide and varied, the scene and emphasis
of the novel are particular. The prevailing atmosphere
aboard the *Fidèle* is one of chicanery and fraud. In making literary use of a host of criminal tactics and in pre-

senting various types of confidence men, Melville chose to portray an aspect of American society dominated by deceit. Moreover, as the novel progresses, the variations on this theme of deceit become increasingly complex until, with the appearance of Frank Goodman, the method and manner of deception are almost playful.

What begins as simple venality ultimately results in a sort of gamesmanship. The humiliating antics of the beggar, Black Guinea, are soon replaced by more sophisticated swindles. Rather than the simple appeal to one's charitable instincts, the confidence games practiced by the president of the Black Rapids Coal Company assume some knowledge of financial investment. In chapter 21, the herb doctor argues the virtues of "Dame Natur," his herbal medicines being but the by-product of a natural beneficence. And in chapter 22, the P.I.O. man claims to conduct his business according to strict "philosophical" principles and involves his victim in a complicated form of analogical reasoning. Nevertheless, all of these confidence men successfully swindle their victims for varying amounts of money.

With the cosmopolitan, however, financial gain appears to be secondary to merely inspiring confidence. Frank Goodman's only successful swindle is the duping of the barber for the trifling price of a shave. Rather than wishing to relieve his victims of their money, the cosmopolitan seems content to expose the outright hypocrisy of Charlie Noble or the unconscious hypocrisy of Mark Winsome and Egbert. The earnest appeals for a loan made by the man with the weed are replaced in the latter half of the book by appeals for money made by one "hypothetical" friend to another. In the character of Frank Goodman, Melville presented a rarified form of confidence man, more fond of the confidence game itself than any possible rewards that might result. This "hypothetical" character of the second half of the novel would seem to indicate that Melville had shifted the emphasis of his book to an amused, often playful consideration of his confidence man as rascal and mischiefmaker.

With remarkable variety, Melville made literary use of many types of swindlers. He found in the confidence man a character representative of the age. And, perhaps following the precedents of *White-Jacket* and *Moby-Dick*, in which the ship figured as a microcosm, he placed that character aboard the *Fidèle*, where he might consider the world in a riverboat. It was aboard a riverboat that such confidence men conventionally operated and where "that multiform pilgrim species, man" (9) might be expected to assemble for a single voyage.

The *Fidèle* provided a fitting stage for the author's central character. However, as the many separate confrontations show, Melville presented in his novel not one but several confidence men, each practicing a special form of confidence game; but, in doing so, he created a confusion in which the identity of his original confidence man has been lost. Is there a central character who appears in the book from beginning to end and gives it a unity that many readers have failed to observe? And, if so, what are his successive appearances in his masquerade? There is no consensus among readers and critics that provides a firm answer to these questions. It is the aim of the following chapter, therefore, to identify the single dominant character and his various masquerades and to show that he provided not only the title for Melville's book but an intellectual and structural framework for it as well.

George Caleb Bingham, *Dandy,* ca. 1849.
Nelson Gallery—Atkins Museum (Nelson Fund).

Chapter 3

Melville's Antihero

In fleshing out his novel, Melville made "literary use" of a great many confidence-man types and of a variety of contemporary criminal schemes. He at least suggested that some characters, such as the transcendentalists Egbert and Mark Winsome, were unwitting confidence men. And he had satirically compared the tactics of outright swindlers to the practices of socially acceptable types. The net effect of the author's efforts in this direction was to create a pervasive atmosphere of chicanery and venality, of hypocrisy and self-deception. The decks of the *Fidèle* are crowded with swindlers and frauds of one sort or another, but the identity of the single confidence man, in his several disguises, to whom the title of the novel refers, remains in some doubt.[1] This chapter will identify the confidence man as a single figure who assumes eight separate disguises, which constitute his "masquerade." Moreover, Melville invested the masquerade itself with a special "significance" and, in turn, this masquerade provided the author with an almost formulaic structural pattern for his book.

Strangely, the question of the confidence man's identity, a question so fundamental to an understanding of the novel, is not easily answered. And apparently, Melville was not especially anxious to help his readers identify his title character: the term *confidence-man* is used only twice in the novel—in the title and, ambiguously, in the concluding chapter. Nevertheless, the book's subtitle, *His Masquerade,* indicates that the confidence man is a single figure. Consequently, many readers have searched the pages of this puzzling book for reliable clues that would identify the disguises of the confidence man. However, critical opinion is by no means unanimous as to

49

which characters aboard the riverboat are actually the title character in disguise.

There is what Philip Drew has called a "received view" on this particular point.[2] This view is represented by Elizabeth Foster, James Miller, and others and assumes that the confidence man masquerades in the following disguises: Black Guinea; John Ringman, the "man with the weed"; the man in gray; Mr. Truman, the president of the Black Rapids Coal Company; the herb doctor; the P.I.O. man; and Frank Goodman, the cosmopolitan. (The mute in cream colors poses a special problem; Foster and Miller deny that he is the confidence man in disguise, but others believe that he too participates in the masquerade.) However, as Drew has observed, there is no evidence to support this view other than the fact that these characters appear successively, never together, and that they all seem to function as confidence men. "Formally," argues Drew, "they are separate people"; it is merely a matter of "convenience" to treat these several confidence men as a single character in disguise.[3]

Strictly speaking, Drew's contention is accurate. However, there are several instances in which at least an implied relation between certain of these characters, if not a single identity, is evident. In chapter 3, for example, Black Guinea manages to secure one of Mr. Roberts's business cards that falls to the deck when the merchant searches his pockets for his purse. In the following chapter, when Ringman introduces himself to his supposed friend, Ringman apparently makes use of the information printed upon that card: "Are you not, sir, Henry Roberts, forwarding merchant of Wheeling, Virginia? Pray, now, if you use the advertisement of business cards, and happen to have one with you, just look at it, and see whether you are not the man I take you for" (19). Similarly, in chapter 21, the herb doctor learns that Pitch, the Missouri bachelor, has been employing boy servants but is now determined to purchase machinery to do his chores. In chapter 22, the same bachelor is approached by a representative of the "Philosophical

Intelligence Office" who appears to have divined that Pitch might be interested in a boy servant:

> "How did you come to dream that I wanted anything in your line, eh?"
> "Oh, respected sir," whined the other, crouching a pace nearer, and, in his obsequiousness, seeming to wag his very coat-tails behind him, shabby though they were, "oh, sir, from long experience, one glance tells me the gentleman who is in need of our humble services." (114)

Of course the relationship between Black Guinea and Ringman, or between the herb doctor and the P.I.O. man, is merely implied; there is no undeniable evidence that any of these confidence men are in collusion or that a single confidence man in masquerade has assumed these various disguises. *The Confidence-Man* is sufficiently ambiguous at every point to make the identification of the central character at least a debatable matter. Nevertheless, even such a skeptical critic as Drew does not deny that there is a single confidence man aboard the *Fidèle* who assumes many disguises; Drew merely wishes to underscore the ambiguity of the novel and to establish that the "received view" rests upon inferential evidence. The generally accepted basis for identifying the characters who represent a central figure in his various disguises is that they meet the following requirements: (1) they must be identifiable as individuals named by Black Guinea as gentlemen who will testify to the beggar's honesty; (2) they must be fraudulent characters; (3) they must appear successively and those appearances must never overlap; and (4) they must occupy a central position in the episodes in which they are presented.

In chapter 3, after the man with the wooden leg has suggested that Guinea's deformity might be a sham, the crowd, who had previously taken a somewhat grotesque pleasure in the beggar's "game of charity," begins to scrutinize the twisted Negro and demand that Black Guinea present "documentary proof" that he is not a fraud. Guinea has no documents that will exculpate

him, "none o' dem waloable papers," but he claims to
have many friends who will testify on his behalf:

> "Oh yes, oh yes, dar is aboard here a werry nice, good ge'mman
> wid a weed, and a ge'mman in a gray coat and white tie,
> what knows all about me; and a ge'mman wid a big book,
> too; and a yarb-doctor; and a ge'mman in a yaller west; and
> a ge'mman wid a brass plate; and a ge'mman in a wiolet
> robe; and a ge'mman as is a sodjer; and ever so many good,
> kind, honest, ge'mmen more aboard what knows me an
> will speak for me. . . ." (13)

Except for the inclusion of the "ge'mman in a yaller
west" and the "ge'mman as is a sodjer," the descriptions
of Black Guinea's "friends" appear to constitute a list of
identifiable characters who meet the other requirements
for the central figure and appear in the required order.
Ringman, who wears a weed as a token of his mourning,
approaches Mr. Roberts immediately after the crippled
beggar has "stumped out of sight" (17). Ringman wan-
ders offstage at the conclusion of chapter 5, and in chapter 6 the representative of the Seminole Widow and Orphan Asylum, dressed in a gray coat and white tie, comes
on the scene. In chapter 9, Mr. Truman, wearing a traveling
cap and carrying a large transfer book for the Black Rapids Coal Company, replaces the man in gray as the central figure. Truman manages to gull a few passengers,
including a sickly miser. The wretched cough of the
miser prompts Truman to recommend the medicine of
his "friend": "I wish my friend, the herb doctor, were
here now; a box of his Omni-Balsamic Reinvigorator
would do you good" (74). He exits at the conclusion of
chapter 15, and the following chapter opens with the
herb doctor in the process of persuading a sick man to
purchase a box of his medicine. The herb doctor hawks
his wares aboard the *Fidèle* with some success, but at
the end of chapter 21 he claims to have reached his
destination, Cape Girardeau, and hurries toward the landing. Chapter 22 opens with the introduction of the representative of the Philosophical Intelligence Office, who

has a small brass plate inscribed with the letters *P.I.O.* hanging by a chain from his neck. The P.I.O. man persuades the skeptical Missouri bachelor that he can supply Pitch with a truly reliable boy servant. The transaction concluded, the P.I.O. man takes his leave under the pretense that he must look up the cook he has located for an innkeeper at Cairo, the next landing. The departure of the P.I.O. man leaves the surly Pitch alone to contemplate his recent encounter. But in chapter 24, Pitch is approached by Frank Goodman, the cosmopolitan, whom Pitch believes to be yet another "metaphysical scamp" (136). It is this character who retains the center stage for the remainder of the novel. Although Goodman does not wear a "wiolet robe," he does sport a "vesture barred with various hues" and a "smoking-cap of regal purple" (131). Presumably, Goodman is the man to whom Guinea referred as dressed in a "wiolet robe."

Black Guinea's list of friends, therefore, takes on a singular significance, for it has generally been regarded as the most reliable indication of Melville's intention for the masquerade of the title character. Including Black Guinea himself, the list seems to indicate that the confidence man masquerades as seven distinct figures, each of whom practices a special but recognizable form of confidence game. Melville might rely on his readers to recognize current swindles as they were practiced by such figures as a sponsor for a charity, a peddler of fraudulent stocks, a quack doctor, or a representative of an Intelligence Office;[4] and he might even assume that many readers would recognize the resemblance of the man with the weed and the cosmopolitan, in their blunt appeals for confidence, to the original rogue who had prompted the creation of the term *confidence man* in 1849.

Two additional characters on Guinea's list are the gentleman in a "yaller west" and the man "as is a sodjer," who, in his proper order, should follow Frank Goodman. The book ends without his appearance, but the omission is obscured by the fact that a man who claims to have been a soldier appears: the crippled Happy Tom, who claims to have been wounded in the Mexican War and wins the sympathy of others by appealing to their sense of patriotism. And the man in the yellow vest does not appear at all unless there is a residual suggestion of him in Charlie Noble, the Mississippi operator. Although Noble does not wear a yellow vest, he does sport a "violet vest, sending up sunset hues to a countenance betokening a kind of bilious habit" (139). As Elizabeth Foster has suggested, "whatever Melville had in mind about the yellow vest may have been well enough represented by the 'sunset hues' and a bilious face."[5]

Although both characters are types of confidence men, they could not have participated in the central character's masquerade because both have encounters with characters who might more reasonably be expected to be the title character in disguise. Happy Tom, "the soldier of fortune," has a lengthy conversation with the herb doctor, and Charlie Noble conducts an even longer interview with the cosmopolitan. Moreover, the appearance of the herb doctor precedes that of the soldier of fortune, and the herb doctor remains after the soldier has made his exit; this is also the case with the cosmopolitan, who encounters Mark Winsome just after Charlie Noble has bid farewell.

The somewhat disparate episodes that constitute the action of Melville's book are held together by the presence of the title character in masquerade. Although a contemporary reviewer might refuse *The Confidence-Man* the status of a novel on the grounds that it is nothing more than "forty-five conversations held on board a steamer, conducted by personages who might pass for the errata of creation," those conversations are nevertheless given coherence by the continued presence of the title character, in one disguise or another, throughout the book.[6] Charlie Noble and the soldier of fortune are merely passengers, among a great variety of passengers, whom the confidence man happens to encounter aboard the *Fidèle*. Neither the soldier of fortune nor

Charlie Noble seems to suspect his respective interlocutor for a confidence man. Happy Tom privately confesses
to the herb doctor that he is a veteran of the Tombs of
New York City rather than of a battlefield in Mexico;
and neither the herb doctor nor the soldier of fortune
betrays any previous familiarity with the other. Similarly, Charlie Noble takes the cosmopolitan for a possible
victim rather than a fellow swindler. Obviously, the confidence man is not in collusion with either of these
men.

The puzzling discrepancies in Guinea's list—the fact
that neither Happy Tom nor Charlie Noble is part of the
confidence man's masquerade; the fact that neither character appears in the order suggested by the list; and the
apparent fact that the confidence man is not personally
acquainted with either character—have led some to believe that the inclusion of the soldier and the man with
the yellow vest evidences carelessness or forgetfulness
on the part of the author. That is, Guinea's list of friends
seems to indicate Melville's earliest intention for the
confidence man's masquerade; presumably Melville had
originally intended to have the confidence man masquerade as a soldier and as a gentleman in a yellow vest, but
the author either forgot or altered his plan in the process
of composition.[7] Moreover, the apparent reference to
the cosmopolitan as the man in a "wiolet robe" additionally suggests that Melville may have modified his
original conception of this particular disguise. At any
rate, the author did not provide that character with such
a robe.

Nevertheless, excluding the soldier of fortune and Charlie Noble, it seems reasonable to assume that the confidence man masquerades as Black Guinea and, in later
chapters, as Guinea's "friends." Apparently, Melville
had conceived of his central character as a distinct figure who might convincingly play many roles. The title
character emerges as one who is neither in collusion
with the other swindlers aboard the *Fidèle* nor an unwitting hypocrite and fraud, such as Winsome and Eg-

bert. Rather, he is a deceiver who is not only capable of assuming many dissimilar disguises but who might also assume many attitudes. The melancholy man with the weed in no way suggests the optimism of the cosmopolitan; the sprightly gait of the man with the traveling cap does not recall the twisted beggar Guinea; nor does the audacious herb doctor resemble the fawning P.I.O. man. However, though the confidence man might pose as very different characters, the appearance of the deaf-mute in the opening chapters of the novel presents another, rather special problem because his apparent innocence seems to be contrary to the fraudulent aims of a confidence man.

This man in "cream colors" with "flaxen hair," who evenly pursues the "path of duty" (3) and appears to be so "singularly innocent" (4), has puzzled a great many readers of *The Confidence-Man.* Superficially at least, the mute's humble appearance and mild demeanor, coupled with his plea for the observance of St. Paul's message of charity, would seem to indicate that the mute's nature is antithetical to that of a confidence man. Indeed, Elizabeth Foster has discounted the possibility that the mute might be the confidence man in disguise: "Melville clearly differentiates between [the mute] and the Confidence Man: he is innocent of fraud; he is unequivocal; he is not on the Negro's list of Confidence Men."[8]

Some have disputed the mute's innocence, however. H. Bruce Franklin and Daniel Hoffman believe that the mute is guilty of fraud, at least to the extent of reminding certain passengers aboard the *Fidèle* of their duty as Christians to be charitable.[9] In fact, the "charitable lady" who donates twenty dollars to the Widow and Orphan Asylum for Seminoles had been reading I Corinthians 13 previous to her encounter with the man in gray. And, as the narrator points out, the lady's attention to this portion of Scripture "might have recently been turned, by witnessing the scene of the monitory mute and his slate" (43).

Daniel Hoffman has additionally suggested that Melville's familiarity with Cotton Mather's *Magnalia Christi Americani*, which describes many "Wolves in sheeps cloathing," might have inspired the author to create such an impostor for his novel.[10] More likely, however, Melville probably patterned his man in cream colors after contemporary confidence men. It was not uncommon for swindlers to pose as deaf-mutes; William Avery Rockefeller had done so, and apparently an impostor claiming to be Melville himself had pretended muteness.[11] Mark Twain was also probably familiar with this popular method of deception, for many years later, in *Huckleberry Finn* (1884), he would have one of his confidence men, the duke, pretend to be deaf and dumb. Though a deaf-mute confidence man may not have been as generally familiar to readers as a fraudulent beggar or an herb doctor, he would nevertheless be an identifiable type of confidence man who practiced a known form of deception.

The mute in cream colors is also the central figure in the chapters in which he appears, as are the other characters who represent the confidence man in masquerade. Although the mute is not included in Guinea's list—an omission Elizabeth Foster believes significant—he nevertheless might reasonably be expected to participate in the masquerade from the mere fact that he is the focal point of the opening chapters. And, as with the other figures who appear to be the confidence man in disguise, the disappearance of the mute is immediately followed by the appearance of Black Guinea in chapter 3.

All told, then, the masquerade would seem to consist of eight, rather than seven disguises. Despite his apparent innocence, the mute has a place in the confidence man's masquerade along with Black Guinea and six others on his list: John Ringman, Mr. Truman, the man in gray, the herb doctor, the P.I.O. man, and Frank Goodman.

In his masquerade, Melville's confidence man assumes the roles of most of the contemporary types of confidence men that we have surveyed in chapter 2. Apparently the author wished to make his central character a comprehensive, symbolic figure who might play the parts of a multitude of conventional swindlers and practice many recognized forms of fraud and deception. Rather than a character governed by a single ruling passion, Melville's antihero became a character representative of the times, and the author placed him on a Mississippi riverboat, where such confidence men were a commonplace.

However, in creating such a versatile swindler, the author necessarily risked producing a very enigmatic character. Apart from their use of confidence-man techniques, the several manifestations of the confidence man have very little in common. Taken together, these eight figures fail to give the impression of a single character who merely assumes a variety of disguises. The "fair" face of the man in cream colors is inconsistent with the robust appearance of the man in gray. The twisted deformity of Black Guinea and the groveling attitude of the "baker-kneed" P.I.O. man sharply contrast with the brisk stride of the man in the traveling cap and the athletic pose of the cosmopolitan. Nor does the venality of most of these figures square with the apparent indifference to financial gain of the mute and the cosmopolitan. The mute does not even solicit money, and the cosmopolitan appears more interested in companionship and conversation than in swindling his acquaintances. In short, though the confidence man is presented as a single figure who plays many parts, the discrepancies in behavior, appearance, and motive seem too great to reveal a single character behind each consecutive mask.

The protean nature of Melville's confidence man, his ability to play so many dissimilar parts convincingly, suggests a mythological figure. His ability to deceive the same passenger in several different disguises, as he does the merchant and Pitch, and to appear deformed and unhealthy, sound and robust with such ease and plausibility suggests that he is no ordinary mortal. As a result of the incongruent nature of the confidence man, many critics have viewed the central character as not merely an extraordinary but as a supernatural figure. Thus, the figures in disguise are usually seen as "avatars" of good or evil rather than as merely deceptive swindlers. Elizabeth Foster, for example, has discounted the "relevance" of questioning the incongruent nature of the confidence man, since a proper understanding of the novel demands that the reader descend to Melville's "little lower layer" in which the title character is an allegorical figure, the Devil.[12]

Among those who have pursued this allegorical line of interpretation, however, there has been an inevitable division of opinion. John Shroeder, Hershel Parker, Daniel Hoffman, and others have agreed with Elizabeth Foster that the confidence man is the Devil. On the other hand, some critics, such as Leslie Fiedler, Lawrance Thompson, and Malcolm O. Magaw, have preferred to treat the confidence man as a Christ-figure or as an embodiment of God.[13] It appears, though, that the Devil's party has clearly gained the ascendancy in this critical controversy—to such an extent, in fact, that Hershel Parker could claim in the foreword to the Norton Critical Edition of *The Confidence-Man* that this view is part of the "standard line of interpretation."[14]

There are certain obvious advantages in treating *The Confidence-Man* as an allegory in which the central figure is the Devil. First, by investing the confidence man with an identifiable symbolic significance, the victims of the various confidence games practiced by this swindler might be rather precisely measured in accordance with their ability to resist the forces of evil, which is the deception of the confidence man.[15] Second, given Satan's reputation as shape-shifter and evildoer, the incongruous nature of the title character in his various disguises would merely be the result of a supernatural capacity for fraud and deception. Finally, a great many of the episodes and much of the imagery in the novel might successfully be brought together and characterized as "satanic" or "devilish."

We might briefly enumerate some of the results of

this final advantage. Elizabeth Foster, remarking upon the frequent allusions the confidence man makes to the Bible throughout the novel, claims that this is perfectly consistent with his character since the Devil is apt to quote Scripture for his own purposes. She also notes the emphasis on the terms *original* and *original genius* in reference to the confidence man; and she suggests that perhaps this emphasis hints that the confidence man is a "manifestation of an original or primal force in the universe"—namely, the "evil at the heart of things."[16] John Shroeder argues that the occasional snake imagery, particularly in reference to the confidence man, is reliable evidence that the confidence man is the Devil.[17] Daniel Hoffman, following this line of interpretation, claims that Melville succeeded in "translating the folk and theological significance of witch-craft into believable contemporary terms."[18] And Hershel Parker, in agreement with Foster and Shroeder, maintains that Melville deliberately referred to Indians in the novel in such a way that they too are symbolically Devils, and consequently, in the context of the novel, there is a similarity of the "dedication to Indian-hating to the dedication to Christianity."[19]

An interpretation of *The Confidence-Man* as an allegory in which the central character is the Devil is plausible, and it is a theory ably defended by its proponents. Certainly such a theory conveniently explains many aspects of the novel that some readers have found troublesome, particularly the incongruous nature of the confidence man in his many disguises. But, in the end, it is too easy a solution. It oversimplifies a book that even the critics who identify the confidence man with the Devil find too complex for an allegorical interpretation based on that identification. As we shall see when considering the relationship of Melville's character to Milton's Satan, the confidence man could have devilish qualities on occasion without being consistently a Devil. He could play a variety of symbolic roles as readily as he could play his many realistic ones. *The Confidence-*

Man, perhaps to a greater degree than *Pierre*, is a book of
ambiguities; and its ambiguous title character possessed
a dramatic flexibility that permitted his creator to explore through him a wideranging suggestiveness too complex for simple allegory, yet which ultimately resulted
in a far more provocative book. Melville's character could
not only quote Scripture but also act it out for his purpose; in doing so, he played a part that is almost completely opposite to the role suggested by the Devil theory but that enables the reader to find a much greater
coherence in the book.

That part begins in the first chapter when the mute in
cream colors traces the following scriptural passages on
his slate:

> Charity thinketh no evil.
> Charity suffereth long, and is kind.
> Charity endureth all things.
> Charity believeth all things.
> Charity never faileth. (4–5)

These are, of course, almost exact quotations from chapter 13 of Paul's first epistle to the Corinthians, and the
irony of their use as an introduction to such a book as
The Confidence-Man has been generally recognized. The
concluding verse of this chapter ("And now abideth faith,
hope, and charity, these three; but the greatest of these
is charity") also contributes to the irony, because throughout the book the confidence man pleads for faith, preys
upon hope, and preaches the gospel of charity. For an
understanding of the confidence man and the various
aspects of his masquerade in his most important suggestive role, however, the concluding verse of the twelfth
chapter of I Corinthians is even more significant.

In this chapter Paul makes a special plea for unity in
the church. Although its body has many members, he
argues, these are all parts of the same body and spirit.
Paul writes that members of the church, as with members of the body, may serve Christ in many ways, and he
lists certain types of the faithful whom God has appointed

to the church: "And God hath set some in the church, first *apostles*, secondarily *prophets*, thirdly *teachers*, after that *miracles*, then gifts of *healings, helps, governments, diversities of tongues*" (I Corinthians 12:28; italics mine). These are the chosen offices of the church: apostles, prophets, teachers, workers of miracles, healers, helpers, governors, and those with the gift of tongues. Although Melville was not strictly obedient to the order presented by St. Paul, he seems to have used this passage in providing his confidence man with suggestive disguises.[20]

If he did, the confidence man should first appear as an apostolic figure. An apostle is by definition a messenger of God sent to preach the gospel. When the mute scratches Paul's message of charity on his slate, he is in effect an apostle delivering the gospel to that crowd of "pilgrims" aboard the *Fidèle*. Perhaps with deliberate irony, Melville made this messenger a deaf-mute who, unable to preach, is reduced to scribbling on a slate, uttering "a peculiar inarticulate moan, and a pathetic telegraphing of his fingers" (6). It is the type of irony that echoes the Plinlimmon chapters of *Pierre*, in which the voice of God is likened to a "profound Silence."[21]

Disguised as the impoverished Black Guinea, the confidence man in his second role betrays his powers of prophecy. This twisted black beggar performs his pathetic shuffle and plays his tambourine in hopes that sympathetic passengers will toss a few coins his way. The crowd willingly enters into the "game of charity" until the man with a wooden leg arouses their suspicions by suggesting that Guinea is a fraud. In response to the crowd's demands for documentary proof of his authenticity, the beggar offers his list of "friends" as men who will testify to his honesty. As has already been pointed out, Guinea's list includes all the future disguises of the confidence man and is clearly prophetic, providing the essential clue to the identity of the character who unifies the entire book. The fact that Black Guinea's prophecy is not completly fulfilled does not invalidate his role as prophet.

The confidence man next assumes the disguise of John Ringman, "the man with the weed," and in this role the confidence man acts the part of teacher. When Ringman seeks to "renew" his acquaintance with Mr. Roberts, the merchant, he tries to instruct his would-be victim about the inconstancy of human memory, a condition that might account for Roberts's failure to recollect his former relationship with Ringman. His explicit identification of himself as a teacher, however, is in chapter 5 when he confronts the college sophomore. The collegian carries "a small book bound in Roman vellum," a fact that does not pass unnoticed by Ringman. When he observes that the volume is by Tacitus, he immediately begins to lecture on the "moral poison" espoused by the ancient cynic. He offers to throw this unhealthy volume overboard, but the sophomore begins to protest. Before the collegian can voice his objection, however, the man with the weed cuts him off: "Not a word; I know just what is in your mind, and that is just what I am speaking to. Yes, *learn from me* that, though the sorrows of the world are great, its wickedness—that is, its ugliness—is small" (26; italics mine).

Continuing his masquerade, the confidence man, now disguised as the "man in gray," pretends to represent the Widow and Orphan Asylum for Seminole Indians. After soliciting a contribution to this charity from the Methodist minister, the man in gray introduces himself to the man with gold sleeve buttons. In addition to serving as a representative for the Widow and Orphan Asylum, the confidence man claims to be the inventor of the miraculous Protean easy chair and the author of a prospectus for the World's Charity. By acquiring the contribution of one dollar per year for fourteen years from every living person, the man in gray claims that the World's Charity will raise "eleven thousand two hundred millions" of dollars practically overnight. The man with gold sleeve buttons is evidently impressed by the magnitude of this project, but he has certain reservations: "Sharing the character of your general project, these things, I take it, are rather *examples of wonders that were to be wished*, than wonders that will happen" (41; italics mine). The ever-optimistic man in gray is immune to such criticism, however: "And is the age of wonders passed? Is the world too old? Is it barren? Think of Sarah" (41). The man in gray, then, claims to be a worker of miracles, the fourth type of the faithful as described by St. Paul.

According to the Pauline order, the confidence man's fifth masquerade should be as a healer. However, Melville altered this order (as the mute had altered the biblical order of assertions on his slate), and the man with the traveling cap appears to fulfill the role of governor, rather than healer. The translators of the King James Bible were not absolutely clear about the meaning of *governments*. Other versions of the Bible clarify the meaning of the term somewhat by translating it as *administrator*, and this was probably the way Melville understood the word. At any rate, the man with the traveling cap, president and transfer agent for the Black Rapids Coal Company, certainly qualifies as an administrative type.

In his sixth disguise, the confidence man appears as the audacious and talkative "Yarb-Doctor." As a natural bone-setter and peddler of the Omni-Balsamic Reinvigorator and the Samaritan Pain Dissuader, the herb doctor unquestionably masquerades as one with gifts of healing.

In his next disguise, the confidence man masquerades as a representative of the "Philosophical Intelligence Office." In this role he plays the part of helper. The P.I.O. man claims to be able to supply prospective employers with reliable servants, but when he offers to "accommodate" the Missouri bachelor with a boy, the discerning Pitch curtly refuses this type of aid: "Accommodate? Pray, no doubt you could accommodate me with a bosom-friend too, couldn't you? Accommodate! Obliging word accommodate: there's accommodation notes now, where one accommodates another with a loan, and if he don't pay it pretty quickly, accommodates him with a chain to his foot. Accommodate! God forbid that I should ever be accommodated" (115–16).

In the second half of the book, Frank Goodman, the cosmopolitan, masquerades as one who speaks in a "diversity of tongues" (and with "the tongues of men and of angels"); Goodman speaks with a voice as "sweet as a seraph's" (130), and he describes himself as a "true citizen of the world," a "catholic man" (132–33). Presumably well traveled and fluent in various languages, the cosmopolitan is a "taster of races" and delights in his fellowman whether he be served up "à la Pole, or à la Moor, à la Ladrone, or à la Yankee" (133). Pitch apparently considers his talk nonsense and associates him with the members of the religious sects (such as the Shakers, with whom Melville was familiar) who professed to "speak in tongues," for he says that the cosmopolitan has been made in the likeness of "the great chimpanzee" and resembles the pantomimist Marzetti and "other chatterers" (132).[22]

By chapter 24, the confidence man's masquerade has come full circle. He began his ruse as a deaf-mute apostle and returns in his final disguise as an apostle of charity who chatters like a nineteenth-century pantomimist. This provides a unity to the book that is not otherwise evident, but it also raises certain questions. Should *The Confidence-Man* be considered primarily if not entirely as a satire on the Christian tradition, which is exemplified by St. Paul's appeal to the Corinthians to practice the virtues of faith, hope, and charity and his implied plea to have confidence in those members of the congregation blessed with special gifts? Was the unity we have found in the book a part of Melville's original plan for it?

The answer to the first question must be held in abeyance until we have considered other suggestive or symbolic roles played by the central character, but two observations are pertinent here. One is that a simple satiric theory, like the allegorical devil theory, does not do justice to the richness of a novel that every sympathetic reader has found exceedingly complex. The other is that we have very little evidence of what Melville had in mind or put on paper before his manuscript was prepared for the printer and public scrutiny. This little evidence consists entirely of a surviving manuscript version of chapter 14 that was considerably revised for publication. In her careful study of these revisions, Elizabeth Foster has conclusively demonstrated that Melville toned down his sacrilegious impulses;[23] and on this basis it seems legitimate to assume that there was more antireligious feeling beneath the surface of the book than is readily apparent in the printed text. The extent and the details of this, however, are something we do not know.

An answer to the second question must be more speculative and based on a different sort of evidence, but some attempt to deal with it is necessary because of the many inconsistencies within the book. The most important of these are the differences between the characters mentioned in Black Guinea's prophetic list and the actual masquerades of the central confidence man, the introduction of the mute before Black Guinea makes his introductory prophecy, and such parallelisms with St. Paul's officers of the church as may be observed in the belated identification of John Ringman as a teacher, the miraculous aspirations of the representative of the Widow and Orphan Society, and the identification of the company president as a "governor." These inconsistencies suggest that Melville's imagination was as flexible in his approach to this book as it had been in *Moby-Dick*, and *Pierre*, and as it had been forced to be in *Mardi*. It seems especially unlikely that he composed Black Guinea's list when all the events he was to use in his novel were clearly in his mind. On the contrary, it would appear that Melville's imagination created many of the specific incidents in his book while he was in the process of writing, and that he simply failed in *The*

Confidence-Man, as he had in *Moby-Dick*, to reconcile all his foreshadowings with the actual development of his narrative.

For this reason, the temporal relationship between the composition of *The Confidence-Man* and Melville's attention to the twelfth and thirteenth chapters of I Corinthians becomes an interesting matter for speculation. Melville's familiarity with the Bible is amply demonstrated in his books, especially from *Moby-Dick* onward, and the annotations in the copy he obtained in the spring of 1850[24] indicate that he attained some of this familiarity in the midst of his active writing career. But whether he read the Bible systematically or impulsively is unknown. Within the Melville household, however, there was probably a certain amount of systematic Bible reading directed by the Episcopal *Book of Common Prayer*. Melville bought two copies of the Prayer Book in 1849, and his Aunt Mary gave him another copy on 25 September 1850, soon after he had moved to Pittsfield.[25] His sisters attended Episcopal services when they were living in New York City, and it is not unlikely that in Pittsfield some members of the family read the weekly (if not the daily) lessons, whether or not they were able to attend church.[26]

In the mid-nineteenth-century order of service, the evening New Testament lesson for the second Sunday after Epiphany (20 January 1856) was the thirteenth chapter of I Corinthians, and it could have been brought to Melville's special attention either by discussion or by the custom of reading aloud, which was practiced in the household.[27] The possibility of such an occurrence invites further speculation about the complex of biblical lessons for that day. The morning lesson from the New Testament was a verse from the Gospel According to St. John (1:29): "The next day John seeth Jesus coming unto him, and saith, Behold the Lamb of God, which taketh away the sin of the world." The morning lesson from the Old Testament was from Isaiah 51 and included a suggestive passage in which that evangelical prophet bewailed the woes of Jerusalem: "There is none to guide her among all the sons she hath brought forth; neither is there any that taketh her by the hand of all the sons that she hath brought up" (51:18). The evening lesson consisted of I Corinthians 13 and part of chapter 52 from Isaiah (1–13). In the fifty-second chapter Isaiah praises one who might deliver them: "How beautiful upon the mountains are the feet of him that bringeth good tidings, that publisheth peace; that bringeth good tidings of good, that publisheth salvation; that saith unto Zion, Thy God reigneth!" (52:7).

Taken together, these passages seem to have a germinal relationship to the unifying idea of *The Confidence-Man*. I Corinthians 13 is the chapter in the Bible from which the author quotes most extensively and to which he most frequently refers; and chapter 12, of which it is a continuation, provides parallels to the title character's disguises. The "Lamb of God" in John 1:29 suggests the "lamb-like figure" (6) of the mute in the cream-colored suit and fleecy white hat; and it is the mute who "publisheth" peace and salvation by writing on his slate. And the verse from the fifty-first chapter of Isaiah suggests the irony of a holy community that can find no one among its members who can be trusted to guide the others.

This is speculation, of course, but the hypothesis that Melville's unifying idea came to him after the composition of his book was well under way suggests an explanation for a number of the puzzles presented by the text and at least one of the surviving manuscript fragments. It would explain why he dropped the soldier and the gentleman in the yellow vest from the list of characters in the confidence man's masquerade and added the lamblike figure of the mute. Such changes would be necessary for whatever narrative coherence is provided by his ironic adaptation of the confidence man's masquerade to the pattern suggested by St. Paul's types of the faithful. The imposition of a pattern upon an existing narrative might also explain why the central character sometimes undergoes radical transformations in the same disguise. John Ringman throws off his air of melancholy and "seemed almost transformed into another being" (25) just before he approaches the college sophomore—the episode in which he clearly identifies himself as a teacher. Similarly, the man in gray "resumes his original air" (43) just after proposing to the man in gold sleeve buttons his miraculous scheme for the World's Charity, thus identifying himself as a worker of miracles. Melville may have revised or inserted these episodes in order to bring these two figures into line with the Pauline pattern. Melville also may have been belated in his recognition of the qualities of a governor or administrator in the president of the Black Rapids Coal Company and left him in his original position in the narrative without trying to bring him into line as the occupant of the seventh place in St. Paul's list. The herb doctor, as a fraudulent healer, and the man from the Philosophical Intelligence Office, as a fraudulent helper, fitted into the pattern from their inception; but they are both such conventional frauds that they were not necessarily conceived under the influence of the biblical pattern. In short, six of the confidence man's disguises (including Black Guinea) could have been adapted to the unifying scheme found in I Corinthians 12:28. Only the lamblike mute and the cosmopolitan, Frank Goodman, seem to owe their origin to the biblical influence.

The mute, who provides the substance of chapter 1 and is the subject of comments in chapter 2, is more than a simple puzzle. Although he "cons" no one out of anything, he is an apostle of charity who, in contrast to the barber and his sign of No Trust, advocates faith, thereby setting the ironic stage that Melville's antihero occupies while he preys upon these Christian virtues as well as upon the occasional hopes of his victims. Without his appearance at the beginning, the whole tone of the book would be different. That would be especially apparent if one imagines the book opening with a chapter like the manuscript fragment entitled "The River," which seems to have been the author's original or alternate draft of his beginning. With this, the emphasis would have been upon a voyage following the course of the Mississippi from the Falls of St. Anthony toward the sea—as Melville himself had probably followed it to the mouth of the Ohio in 1840, as far as the *Fidèle* gets in the course of his book. Since this is the structural pattern he followed in the first six of his eight earlier novels, it is not improbable that Melville should have planned his book in this way, only to find that without the unifying device of a first-person narrator his story was falling to pieces as a series of apparently unconnected incidents. His use of the mute instead created a situation that enabled him to achieve unity through the character of the confidence man and make an ironic commentary on the Christian virtues and the Christian callings as he had found them set forth by Paul. This is the same sort of unity he found (as he indicated in the next-to-last chapter of the novel) in *Hamlet, Don Quixote,* and, somewhat curiously, *Paradise Lost.* An original character in literature, he was to say, was an extraordinarily rare occurrence, but "in certain minds," he felt sure, "there follows upon the adequate conception of such a character, an effect, in its way, akin to that which in Genesis attends upon the beginning of things" (239).

Melville realized that an author who achieved such a character had to have much knowledge and "much luck" (239). Nearly a century later, Ernest Hemingway would express similar feelings about character creation, though he distinguished between mere characters and "living people" in literature: "People in a novel, not skillfully constructed *characters,* must be projected from the writer's assimilated experience, from his knowledge, from his head, from his heart and from all there is of him. If he ever has luck as well as seriousness and gets them out entire they will have more than one dimension and they will last a long time."[28] Apparently Melville felt that the creations of Hamlet, Don Quixote, and Milton's Satan were, in part, the products of such "luck." And he may have felt fortunate to have "found" an original character himself in a contemporary swindler.

Yet Melville's confidence man in most of his manifestations was hardly an original character. His prototype had been widely hailed as an "original" in his actions, and the name was new, but the disguises Melville's confidence man assumed were a familiar part of American society. For that reason, Frank Goodman, his last manifestation, played an extraordinary part in Melville's design. Evidently, the author conceived of the cosmopolitan as a rather different sort of swindler than those he had already portrayed, one whose appeals were made not to individual desires and ambitions, nor to fear or pity or other baser instincts, but to sweet charity and confidence alone. Frank Goodman hawks no wares, promises neither cures nor riches nor aid. Rather, he is a versatile swindler who relies solely on his wit and address and appears less interested in the "take" than in the game itself. Moreover, he moves easily through the strata of humanity aboard the *Fidèle*, ignorant or unminding of fine distinctions of class and learning; he stands upon no ceremonies and with well-traveled aplomb gladhands all those he meets.

He is, in short, the type of confidence man *A Dictionary of the Underworld* identifies as a "man of the world," a nineteenth-century cant expression that may have been in use in Melville's day and familiar to him. The term is defined as any thief who "so loves to style himself, not from any resemblance to the similarly designated personage of polite society, but from the fact of his accomplishments being such that he can follow his profession anywhere."[29] Such a confidence man is an actor. He is one who, unrestrained by either dress or social convention, adapts chameleonlike to the colors of any given situation. Presumably, that sort of rogue would possess those characteristics that Melville attributed to a class of fictional characters and by implication to the cosmopolitan, but that "the proprieties will not allow people to act out themselves with that unreserve permitted to the stage" (182–83). Such a figure would "dress as nobody exactly dresses, talk as nobody exactly talks, act as nobody exactly acts." Though these remarks, contained in chapter 33, have direct application to a consideration of the customary demands of readers of fiction and of fictional characters generally, and though they serve, superficially at least, as a defense of the "unreal" behavior of the cosmopolitan in the previous chapter, Melville's antic character may have in fact derived from the author's attempts to portray a "real" type of swindler. That is, his treatment of Frank Goodman and the imagined "complaints" Melville hears from disbelieving readers may have followed from the dramatic latitude he acquired when he had his confidence man adopt the role of a more flamboyant and mysterious swindler. Frank Goodman describes himself as a "citizen of the world" (133), claims that life is a "pic-nic *en costume*" (133) in which one must "assume a character," views no man as a "stranger," and ties himself to "no narrow tailor or teacher, but federates, in heart as in costume, something of the various gallantries of men under various suns" (132). These qualities certainly pertain to the type of swindler known as a "man of the world."

Whether the cosmopolitan was conceived first as a conventional type of swindler and his role was later modified by its appropriateness to I Corinthians or whether he was conceived as one who spoke in tongues and was later provided (as presumably the mute, who also seems to have been a late creation, was provided) with a familiar method of swindle in order to mark him as a confidence man is uncertain. In any event, it was in the character of Goodman that Melville sought to create a truly extraordinary sort of rogue that was hardly derivative. Introduced as a man who spoke with the voice of an angel, a cosmopolitan who was at home with many people and presumably able to speak to them in many languages, he qualified as a man with the gift of tongues. Though he had not charity, he cheated no one—except the man of no faith, the barber, who, in a battle of wits on April Fool's Day, lost the price of a single shave. It was the confidence man's masquerade as Frank Goodman that earned him the designation "quite an original," and it was through Goodman, who dominated the second half of the book, that Melville achieved the quality of ironic ambiguity that raised his novel above the level of ordinary social satire. It was mostly in the character of Goodman, too, that Melville's mind ranged through those "significances" derived from literature that modified the satiric and sacrilegious implications of his book by having his confidence man play other suggestive roles.

George Caleb Bingham, *Citizen of Undoubted Worth*, 1847.
Nelson Gallery—Atkins Museum (Nelson Fund).

Chapter 4

Literary Models

Whenever the final conception of the confidence man took shape in Melville's mind, he seems to have had a clear notion by the time he wrote his next-to-last chapter of what he had been trying to do. Rather than being a "yarn" such as his earlier novels had been, his new book was unified by a central character who provided the "skeleton of actual reality" on which the author had built a story "instinct with significance." He had "picked up" his character "in town," a character who had been widely recognized as "original" and whose exploits had prompted the creation of a term new to the language which Melville had adopted as the title of his book. In the first part of his story he had explored the realistic and social significances of his confidence man by placing him on a crowded riverboat, where Mississippi operators were known to practice their swindles, and by allowing him to prey upon the gullible or greedy passengers who made his existence possible. Melville had also imposed on that character a certain symbolic significance by making his various manifestations in masquerade correspond to those individuals within the Christian church to whom St. Paul had attributed special gifts. Melville had not, however, turned his story into a moral or a satiric allegory. On the contrary, chapter 44 reveals that he had a more ambitious aim. He was more interested in creation than in commentary, and the goal he set for himself was a high one. He wished to create in the confidence man's final masquerade as Frank Goodman a character who would rival the most original creations of Milton, Shakespeare, and Cervantes. Melville might create all sorts of "novel" or "striking" characters in the figures whom the title character attempted to swindle, but it was in the confidence man himself that Melville was trying to achieve the originality he admired—although, as we shall see, he was more concerned with emulating the authors than with imitating the characters he mentioned.

Of the three "original characters in fiction"—Hamlet, Don Quixote, and Milton's Satan—only the last plays a role resembling that of a confidence man. This may explain Melville's rather curious reference to him, for not even Blake and other "Satanists" would claim that Milton's character dominated his poem in the same way that Hamlet dominated Shakespeare's play, or Don Quixote dominated Cervantes's novel. In any case, the many satanic references throughout Melville's book suggest that he had the Miltonic character in mind from the beginning, although, as we have noted earlier, this does not mean that Melville's character is an allegorical representative of the Devil.[1] His confidence man may be a cheat and a fraud, but he is not particularly evil by nature. His deceit has no very serious consequences— certainly nothing that would rival Satan's temptation of Eve. And he is not motivated by a passion for revenge or by any notable passion at all. Nevertheless, Milton's Satan is a skillful deceiver who, like Melville's confidence man, masquerades in many disguises.

Melville's general indebtedness to Milton has been cogently argued by Henry F. Pommer in his *Milton and Melville.* In particular, Pommer believes Melville's fascination with Milton's Satan may have exerted considerable influence on the author in his creation of outright villains such as Jackson, Bland, and Claggart and in the creation of his famous rebel, Ahab. Melville's use of Satan in creating these first three characters, suggests Pommer, may have stemmed from a "classical" reaction to Satan; the satanic traits of wickedness, jealousy, and hatred are abundant in these villains. However, Melville may have cultivated a "romantic" reaction to the same character with Ahab, for he emphasized the heroic traits of pride, tyranny, and defiance in the creation of the rebellious Ahab. That Melville's imagination was capable of both classical and romantic reactions to Satan is certain, but he cultivated still a third reaction to Milton's character in creating the confidence man—a sardonic one. And in this third reaction, he chose to emphasize Satan's traits of fraud and deceit; rather than as undiluted villain or as mighty rebel, he sardonically viewed this character as a hellish rogue.[2]

Although Pommer does not suggest that Milton's Satan directly influenced the creation of Melville's confidence man, he has found clear echoes of specific lines in *Paradise Lost*, some of them spoken by Satan, in *The Confidence-Man*. For example, the confidence man's boasts for stock in the Black Rapids Coal Company are clearly derived from the boasts of Satan:

> There will be a reaction; from the stock's descent its rise will be higher than from no fall, the holders trusting themselves to fear no second fate. (22)

> From this descent
> Celestial virtues rising, will appear
> More glorious and more dread than from no fall,
> And trust themselves to fear no second fate.
> (*Paradise Lost* 2.14–17)[3]

Allusions such as this, coupled with Melville's mention of Milton's Satan as a thoroughly original character, prove that Satan was in the author's thoughts during the composition of the novel.

Satan's humiliating defeat in heavenly combat prompts Milton's villain to exact his revenge by indirection. Satan is a corrupter of innocents, the tempter of God's creations. In this sense, Milton recognized Satan as an "archfelon," the "first grand Thief" (*PL* 4.193). Satan is the archetypal rogue who, having suffered defeat in open combat, settles for a covert war of camouflage and subterfuge: "our better part remains / To work in close design, by fraud or guile / What force effected not" (*PL* 1.645–47). In contrast to the "bandits of Ohio" or the

"pirate of the Mississippi" (4), the confidence man is a
kind of thief who, like Satan, works in "close design";
he is a fox rather than a wolf.

One of the mainstays of Satan's guile is the disguise.
At one point or another in *Paradise Lost*, Satan masquerades as a cherub, a cormorant, a lion, a tiger, a toad, a
mist, and, of course, a serpent. Much like a confidence
man, Satan assumes the disguise in order to gather information necessary to future deceit:

> Then from his lofty stand on that high Tree
> Down he alights among the sportful Herd
> Of those fourfooted kinds, himself now one,
> Now other, as thir shape serv'd best his end
> Nearer to view his prey, and unespi'd
> To mark what of thir state he more might learn
> By word or action markt.
>
> (*PL* 4.395–401)

After learning that the Tree of Knowledge is forbidden
Adam and Eve, the method of his vengeance becomes
clear, and Satan cautions himself: "Yet let me not forget
what I have gained / From thir own mouths" (*PL* 4.511–12).

Melville's rogue also "marks" the state of his would-be
victims. Black Guinea secretly obtains Mr. Roberts's business card, which provides him with the information
necessary to conduct a future swindle in the disguise of
the man with the weed. The president of the Black Rapids Coal Company learns of the miser's sickness and
laments that his friend the herb doctor is not present to
cure him. Shortly afterward, however, the herb doctor
presents himself to the miser and subsequently swindles him for the price of a box of his medicine. Similarly,
the herb doctor learns of the Missourian's need for a boy
servant, and later, disguised as the P.I.O. man, the confidence man claims to be able to supply him with one.

Satan was also the "first / That practiced falsehood
under saintly show" (*PL* 4.121–22). Disguised as a cherub, Satan's hypocritical innocence recalls the appearance of the mute in cream colors:

> And now a stripling Cherub he appears,
> Not of the prime, yet such as in his face
> Youth smil'd Celestial, and to every Limb
> Suitable grace diffus'd so well he feigned.
> $\qquad$ (*PL* 3.636–39)

The mute, too, has an aura of innocence about him, though, like Satan, not of the prime. The deaf-mute's suit, although neither "soiled nor slovenly," has a certain "tossed look, almost linty"; and his aspect is "at once gentle and jaded" (6).[4]

The confidence man, like Satan, "perverts best things / To worst abuse, or to thir meanest use" (*PL* 4.203–4). The confidence man, as Elizabeth Foster has observed, often quotes Scripture to his advantage; and, in tracing passages from I Corinthians 13 upon his slate, the mute softens passengers for future duping.

It is in the disguise of cherub that Satan obtains from Uriel directions to "Adam's abode." And Milton explains why Uriel, though wise, is unsuspicious of the impostor:

> And oft though wisdom wake, suspicion sleeps
> At wisdom's Gate, and to simplicity
> Resigns her charge, while goodness thinks no ill
> Where no ill seems.
> $\qquad$ (*PL* 3.686–89)

In chapter 23, Pitch, the Missouri bachelor, curses himself for a similar simplicity, and in similar language:

> But where was slipped the entering wedge? Philosophy, knowledge, experience—were those trusty knights of the castle recreant? No, but unbeknown to them, the enemy stole on the castle's south side, its genial one, where Suspicion, the warder, parleyed. In fine, his too indulgent, too artless and companionable nature betrayed him. (130)[5]

And Pitch, like Uriel, had been led into this simplicity by an impostor's "sociable chat" (130). Only gradually, however, does Pitch perceive the roguish nature of the P.I.O. man:

> Analogically, he couples the slanting cut of the equivoca-
> tor's coat-tails with the sinister cast in his eye; he weighs
> sly-boot's sleek speech in the light imparted by the oblique
> import of the smooth slope of his worn boot-heels; the
> insinuator's undulating flunkyisms dovetail into those of
> the flunky beast that windeth his way on his belly. (130)

Uriel is also slow to perceive that he has been duped;
but when he gradually recognizes his mistake, he hurries off to Paradise to warn Gabriel that Satan may be on
the grounds.

Melville's character, at least in one instance, also seems
to display Satan's sense of "injur'd merit" (*PL* 1.98). One
journalist complained of the "natural impudence" of
the original confidence man; when he went to observe
the rogue in the Tombs, he noted that the original confidence man had the audacity to ask two visitors to the
prison, "Gentlemen, have either of you a cigar? I am the
Confidence Man."[6] Melville's John Ringman, like the
original confidence man and Milton's Satan, believes
himself a rather superior individual; even as beneficiary
of a charitable loan, he remains haughty "as though
nothing but a proper sense of what he owed himself
swayed him" (23).

However, Melville's rogue, like Milton's, is often willing to swallow his pride and play the parts of those who
are despised and obsequious; he does so when he assumes the roles of the crippled beggar and the shabby,
baker-kneed intelligencer. One of the most puzzling aspects of the original confidence man, as well as Melville's
fictional creation, in fact, was the apparent willingness of
an intelligent and proud man to humble himself before
strangers in exchange for rather paltry prizes. Disguised
as the man in gray, the confidence man proposes that it is
unreasonable to suppose that an intelligent white man
could, or should want to, play a Negro beggar in order to
receive a few coppers.[7] And Pitch is equally disturbed by
the P.I.O. man: "He revolves, but cannot comprehend,
the operation, still less the operator. Was the man a
trickster, it must be more for the love than the lucre.

Two or three dirty dollars the motive to so many nice wiles? And yet how full of mean needs his seeming" (130).

Yet proud Satan is willing to put on the shape of a toad or enter the mouth of a serpent if it enables him to exact his revenge. He complains of his "foul descent," that he is "constrain'd / Into a Beast, and mixt with bestial slime," but he is able to rationalize the descent:

> But what will not Ambition and Revenge
> Descend to? who aspires must down as low
> As high he soar'd obnoxious first or last
> To basest things.
>
> (*PL* 9.168–71)

The confidence man also resembles Satan in his capacity for "persuasive fascination." Both rogues are capable of flattery—Satan flatters Eve in the temptation, as the man in gray flatters the charitable lady in chapter 8. And both characters are fond of the orator's art. The herb doctor shows himself to be particularly adept at oratory when he addresses a group of passengers in a loud, clear voice in chapter 18. Satan, even in the shape of a serpent, manages to rise in delivering his tempting speech to Eve:

> As when of old some Orator renown'd
> In *Athens* or free *Rome*, where Eloquence
> Flourish'd, since mute, to some great cause addrest,
> Stood in himself collected . . .
> So standing, moving, or to highth upgrown
> The Tempter all impassion'd thus began.
>
> (*PL* 9.671–73, 677–78)

Those two tempters, Charlie Noble and the cosmopolitan, show equal respect for the orator's art. In chapter 30, Charlie delivers his poetic eulogy of Noah's press, but before allowing him to begin, the cosmopolitan insists on standing: "Tell me when you are about to begin, . . . for, when at public dinners the press is toasted, I

always drink the toast standing, and shall stand while
you pronounce the panegyric" (166).

Above all, Satan beguiles Eve with false reasoning.
The serpent argues the knowledge-giving virtues of the
forbidden fruit, and his argument is not without its intended effect:

> in her ears the sound
> Yet rung of his persuasive words, impregn'd
> With Reason, to her seeming, and with Truth.
> (*PL* 9.736–38)

The confidence man is also apt to lace his arguments
with words that seem "impregn'd with Reason." As the
herb doctor, he follows a dubious line of reasoning in
speaking unqualified praise for the healing powers of
nature; as the P.I.O. man, he claims to be dedicated to
the analogical mode of reason, which Pitch later describes
as a "fallacious" doctrine (130); and throughout the novel,
the confidence man zealously argues the virtues of complete confidence.

There are, in short, many resemblances between Milton's Satan and Melville's confidence man, some of them
clear-cut and some perhaps farfetched, but this does not
mean that the latter was modeled on his predecessor.
Melville admired Milton's literary achievement and was
influenced by it, but he invested his own with other
literary "significances," at once less obvious and less
superficial than the resemblances to Satan. In particular, Melville seems to have found in diverse Shakespearean characters (not merely Hamlet) many qualities that
would enrich his own creation.

The relationship of Hamlet to Melville's confidence
man is quite different from that of Milton's Satan to
Melville's character. Hamlet is as unlike the confidence
man as a character could be. He is deceived rather than
the deceiver. He assumes no disguise. He tells everything that is known about his private thoughts and feelings, whereas the confidence man reveals nothing about

himself to the reader. Hamlet served as a precedent for
Melville's creation only in that he was an extraordinarily
successful example of the sort of "original character"
Melville was trying to create—one who, Melville felt,
"is like a revolving Drummond light, raying away from
itself all round it" and creating in Shakespeare's mind
"an effect, in its way, akin to that which in Genesis
attends upon the beginning of things" (239). Without
the "adequate conception of such a character" there
could have been no play, just as without the confidence
man, however adequately conceived, there could have
been no novel. Melville might well have considered the
character of Hamlet the creative cause from which Shakespeare's play had finally developed in a way that he himself wanted to emulate in creating his novel.

Although no Hamlet-like character appears in *The
Confidence-Man*, there is a great deal of Shakespeare in
Melville's novel. Raymond Long, in his comprehensive
study of Shakespeare's influence on Melville, observes
that Melville may have used Shakespearean characters
to greater tragic effect elsewhere but used Shakespeare
in *The Confidence-Man* more broadly and more frequently
than in any other novel, for "there are more specific
references to Shakespeare in this book than in both
Moby-Dick and *Pierre* combined."[8] There are direct quotations from or clear echoes of at least eight separate
plays in this novel, and specific mention is made of such
Shakespearean characters as Timon, Jack Cade, Malvolio,
Polonius, and Autolycus in addition to Hamlet. Melville may have first found the name for his riverboat in
Cymbeline (where the heroine, Imogene, masquerades
as the boy Fidele) before he gave it a French accent in
recognition of its appropriateness to the theme of faith
and his use of I Corinthians 12.[9]

Leon Howard, who was the first to comment on the
pervasive influence of Shakespeare on *The Confidence-
Man*, attributed a Shakespearean role to the author himself. With reference to the "fancy dress picnic" in Pittsfield on 7 September 1855, at which Melville was an

onlooker rather than a participant and to which he apparently alluded in chapter 24 of his novel, Howard says that Melville "had Shakespeare's authority for the notion that all the world was a stage on which one man in his time plays many parts, and he himself was of a mind to play the melancholy Jaques."[10] In the second half of the novel, Howard suggests, Melville "dropped the bystanding role of the melancholy Jaques and slipped into the story himself in the character of Touchstone."[11]

Indeed, Melville was to give Frank Goodman the coat of motley that Jaques, envious of the carefree Touchstone, had claimed was his fond wish: "O that I were a fool! I am ambitious for a motley coat" (*As You Like It* 2.7.43). Certainly the dress of the cosmopolitan is as gay and festive as anything Jaques might have desired. And, in having his character "take a part, assume a character, stand ready in a sensible way to play the fool" (133), as Howard further observes, Melville had conceived of an unconventional type of "Mississippi operator," one who might play the part of court jester aboard the *Fidèle*. Thus, the cosmopolitan might serve as a "touchstone to men's hidden faults."[12]

Raymond Long, on the other hand, while admitting the "general Jaques-Timon syndrome which permeates the atmosphere of the entire first part of the book," finds the second half dominated not by Touchstone but by the droll wit and clownish attitude of the refined fool of *Twelfth Night*—Feste.[13] But it is the rogue Autolycus of *A Winter's Tale* whom Long nominates as the prototype of the confidence man as a whole.

The mood of the first half of *The Confidence-Man* is undeniably one of oppressive gloom and cynicism. The melancholy of Jaques is paralleled in the character of John Ringman, who wears a weed as a symbol of his mourning. And the misanthropy of the man with the wooden leg, the distrust of the ailing miser, and the skepticism of Pitch recall the cynical Timon of Athens. Moreover, the misery and suffering that are abundant in the first half of the novel create a prevailing atmosphere

of melancholy, if not outright misanthropy; the *Fidèle*
is more akin to a hospital ship than a showboat in this
part of the novel. The man in cream colors is a deaf-
mute; Guinea is a twisted cripple; the P.I.O. man is
"baker-kneed"; the miser has a wretched cough; the
soldier of fortune is paralyzed; and one surly passenger
sports a wooden leg. However, the mood abruptly shifts
with the appearance of the cosmopolitan. The contrast
is dramatic; Long points out that the only mention of
any physical disability in the second half is a casual
reference to a lame horse in the China Aster story.[14] And
it is against this less oppressive background that the confidence man plays the part of the seemingly wise and
voluble fool.

It is evident in his remarks in chapter 33 that Melville
thought his readers would take Goodman for a fool. The
narrator anticipates objection to the "antics" of the cosmopolitan and fancies that a reader might complain:
"How unreal all this is! Who did ever dress or act like
your cosmopolitan? And who, it might be returned, did
ever dress or act like harlequin?" (182). Almost any Shakespearean fool might be expected to dress and act as the
cosmopolitan, especially, as Long suggests, the clown of
Twelfth Night.

Goodman is frequently likened to the fool. The barber
takes the cosmopolitan for "some dry sort of joker" (226);
and Goodman freely admits that he holds "the folly that
dimples the cheek" above "the wisdom that curdles the
blood" (243). Like any good fool, the cosmopolitan re-
jects the "too-sober view of life" (134); he celebrates the
mirth-giving virtues of wine and the conviviality of a
good cigar. In fact, Frank Goodman admits to Charlie
Noble that he is "something of a funny man now and
then" (181).

Feste's is a droll wit, and he confesses that he is a
"corrupter of words" *(Twelfth Night* 3.1.41). Goodman
is also guilty of frequent drolleries and is particularly
fond of the pun. In a discussion of the word *favor,* for
instance, Mark Winsome claims ignorance of the word

ever signifying "being done good to." However, he has "inklings" that, in his previous life as the "stoic Arrian," a word of that language had an equivalent meaning, to which the cosmopolitan calmly replies, "Would you favor me by explaining?" (194).

Perhaps more significant, in likening his confidence man to a Shakespearean fool, Melville offered a possible explanation for the original confidence man's behavior. The appearance of that daring swindler had prompted many journalists to speculate as to whether he was some kind of genius or some kind of simpleton. Journalists may have believed these alternatives mutually exclusive, but neither Melville nor Shakespeare would necessarily have felt the compulsion to choose between them. Shakespeare's fools were never simpletons. It takes a wise man to play the fool; and Viola's estimation of Feste might apply equally to the confidence man:

> This fellow's wise enough to play the fool;
> And, to do that well, craves a kind of wit:
> He must observe their mood on whom he jests,
> The quality of persons, and the time;
> And, like the haggard, check at every feather
> That comes before his eye. This is a practice
> As full of labour as a wise man's art:
> For folly, that he wisely shows, is fit;
> But wise men, folly-fallen, quite taint their wit.
> (*Twelfth Night* 3.1.67–75)

However foolish the confidence man may pretend to be, he is no dolt. As a "corrupter of words," the confidence man often makes his companions the unwitting butts of his jokes. In a discussion of Polonius's maxims, the cosmopolitan pretends amazement at Charlie's intelligence and delivers a left-handed compliment that actually asserts his own superiority: "I should almost think I was now at length beginning to feel the ill effect of an immature mind, too much consorting with a mature one" (171). Similarly, in his conversation with Mark

Winsome, the cosmopolitan pretends to compliment the erudition of the transcendentalist: "That, in so defining the thing, Proclus set it to modern understandings in the most crystal light it was susceptible of, I will not rashly deny; still, if you could put the definition in words suited to perceptions like mine, I should take it for a favor" (193).

As the *Fidèle*'s court jester, the cosmopolitan, like any Shakespearean fool, delivers poisoned praise to his supposed superiors. But the cosmopolitan is also able to mark "their mood on whom he jests" and have his fun quite undetected. Charlie Noble, for example, is apparently unaware of the drollery involved when the cosmopolitan interrupts Noble's story of Indian hating in order to fill his "calumet" (151). And Mark Winsome is "constitutionally obtuse to the pleasant drollery" involved in the cosmopolitan's punning on the word *operator*. Winsome has just declared Charlie Noble a "Mississippi operator," which offers the cosmopolitan an opportunity to exercise his wit: "An operator, ah? he operates does he? My friend, then, is something like what the Indians call a Great Medicine, is he? He operates, he purges, he drains off the repletions" (196). As Long points out, such drollery is common in the Shakespearean fool.

The cosmopolitan is also apt to expose many a wise man as "folly-fallen." He does so when he anticipates the designs of Charlie Noble and makes his own appeal for a loan, and he catches the barber in a logical contradiction when the latter is defending his doctrine of faces (233). But this is especially true of the cosmopolitan's dealings with the transcendentalists. Goodman exposes the inconsistencies of both the theoretical and the practical aspects of Winsome's philosophy, but both Winsome and Egbert, reminiscent of Emerson, slough off the criticism as the minor complaint of an inferior mind. At last, toward the end of his interview with Egbert, the cosmopolitan's disgust gets the better of him and he openly ridicules the foolish wisdom of Winsome's philosophy: "What your illustrious magian has taught you, any poor, old, broken-down, heart-shrunken dandy might have lisped" (223).

The confidence man as a whole is more knave than fool, however, and it is the character of Autolycus that may have served Melville as a model of roguery. It is evident, at any rate, that Autolycus was in the thoughts of the author, for the cosmopolitan proposes to Charlie Noble that they "canvass [Shakespeare's] characters" (172), but they do not get beyond a consideration of this rogue of *The Winter's Tale.* Ironically, the cosmopolitan, ordinarily a champion of good humor, pretends to disapprove of the humor of Autolycus because it "oils his mischievousness." "The bravadoing mischievousness of Autolycus is slid into the world on humor," he says, "as a pirate schooner, with colors flying, is launched into the sea on greased ways" (172). He might just as well have been talking about himself.

Raymond Long has noted several additional parallels between Shakespeare's happy rogue and Melville's confidence man. Like Autolycus, the confidence man is a "snapper up of unconsidered trifles," and his "revenue is the silly cheat" (*The Winter's Tale* 4.3.24). Black Guinea is literally a snapper up of "paltry coppers"; the P.I.O. man gulls Pitch for a mere three dollars; and the cosmopolitan bilks the barber for the trifling price of a shave. Also, the confidence man, like Autolycus, has "flown over many knavish professions" and "settled only in rogue" (*The Winter's Tale* 4.3.100). Long also observes that the method of both characters is "the inducing of mental lethargy in his victim with the charming of his voice."[15]

Perhaps more important is the fact that Autolycus, like the confidence man, is able to assume various disguises and to dupe the same victim more than once without being recognized. Autolycus dupes the clown of *The Winter's Tale* three times in as many disguises. Similarly, the confidence man gulls the merchant in the disguises of Black Guinea, Mr. Ringman, and the president of the Black Rapids Coal Company. The ailing miser is swindled by the president of the coal company and by the herb doctor, and Pitch has the dubious honor of entertaining the herb doctor, the P.I.O. man, and the cosmopolitan in rapid succession.

Certainly Melville's use of Shakespeare had enriched his novel and added to the significance of his title character. But, if the confidence man as an original character was Melville's "Drummond light," Shakespeare was not the only source of that character's inspiration and energy. Shakespeare contributed more than did Milton to the literary significance of the confidence man, but not even Autolycus is a real prototype. There was something impractical and perhaps idealistic in Melville's character, especially in his last manifestation as Frank Goodman. For an understanding of that something we must turn to the third "original character" the author had held up for admiration—Cervantes's mad knight, Don Quixote—and to what Melville still seems to have considered the "undefinable" substance of madness in the world he was contemplating.[16]

The literary use Melville made of Cervantes was more subtle and more complex than his use of either Milton or Shakespeare and for that reason warrants special attention. He had been familiar with *Don Quixote* for some time. In *White-Jacket*, he had described the character Nord as a "tall, spare, upright figure stalking like Don Quixote among the pigmies of the After-Guard," and Harry Levin has argued persuasively that the book was in his mind when he wrote *Moby-Dick*.[17] Melville may have renewed his acquaintance with *Don Quixote* in July 1854 when Judge Shaw charged out the first three of the Boston Athenaeum's four- or five-volume edition when his son-in-law was probably in town.[18] On 18 September 1855, eleven days after the fancy-dress picnic, he purchased his own copy of *Don Quixote*, the two-volume illustrated Jarvis translation (Philadelphia, 1853), which survives with his annotations.[19] In "The Piazza," probably written in February 1856, he referred to Don Qui-

xote as the "sagest sage that ever lived";[20] and at some
time during his life he wrote a poem about the Knight of
the Woeful Countenance that provides, as we shall see
in the following chapter, an interesting revelation of
Melville's own attitude toward the character. *Don Quixote* was available to the author and fresh in his mind
throughout the composition of *The Confidence-Man*
and remained in his mind during his travels to the Holy
Land immediately after its completion. Melville recorded
in his journal for 26 November 1856 that a white house
among the gardens of Algiers reminded him of the "Story
of the Morisco" in *Don Quixote;* and in the entry for 23
January 1857, he referred to the "Mania" of the mad
Puritan Zionist, Deacon Dickson, as "Quixotism."[21]

Melville seems not only to have reread *Don Quixote*
in 1855 with sympathy and interest, but also to have
studied the methods of its author, for the text is frequently scored and checked, and he kept a running list
of references to the supposed narrator, Cid Hamet, in
the back flyleaf of the second volume. There is evidence, too, that he read the forty-page "memoir" of Cervantes's life by Louis Viardot that introduces Melville's
copy of the novel.[22]

Viardot's account of the life and times of Cervantes
might have proved suggestive to an author accustomed
to recounting and embellishing his own experiences in
his writing. For Viardot's biographical remarks are prefaced with the statement that "many of the allusions to
be found in the works of Cervantes, can only be understood by those acquainted with the events of his life,"
and this edition provided notes identifying those autobiographical references.[23] Moreover, the portrait Viardot
provides describes a writer and circumstances that resemble Melville's own and may have informed, if not
shaped, Melville's rereading of *Don Quixote*.

The psychological process of identification is an altogether mysterious one for reader and writer alike, and
we ought not presume too much about Melville's personal reaction to this novel or its creator. Nevertheless,

a dozen suggestive details in Viardot's introduction make one suspect that Melville felt strong affinity with and sympathy for the Spanish writer. Like Melville, Cervantes was born into a family that had lost its former position and wealth; both were forced to their travels and adventures—Cervantes as soldier, Melville as sailor. Cervantes, too, suffered wounds and captivity, as Melville had in the Marquesas, and when both finally returned to their native countries, they turned to literature for a livelihood. Enjoying at first a popular success, especially with his dramas, Cervantes soon suffered general public neglect and endured at times severe critical abuse. When he came to write *Don Quixote,* he was in debt and responsible for the support of his wife, a daughter, and two sisters, and no doubt felt a certain bitter jealousy toward the authors of inane but popular romances about knight-errantry.

These biographical details tally in part with Melville's own life and his apparent state of mind at the time he was writing *The Confidence-Man:* he was a writer "damned by dollars," abused by critics, neglected by the reading public, and, as we shall see, bitter toward certain popular nineteenth-century writers. But the resemblances between Cervantes's writing methods as identified by Viardot and the ones Melville had used in the past and adopted for this book are even more suggestive. Like Melville, Cervantes was a writer accustomed to basing his fictions upon personal experience, his reading, and a general familiarity with contemporary events. At times, wrote Viardot, his works suffered from the tendency to make his common characters "too erudite, too philosophical, too eloquent," and the "ill regulated fecundity of his genius" often led him to "heap up episode upon episode."[24] Whether or not Melville was self-consciously critical enough to recognize in these comments his own shortcomings as a writer, ever since the publication of *Mardi* he had heard similar complaints about his fiction. And he was sufficiently aware of such complaints to think it necessary to answer the complaints of an imag-

ined reader about the peculiar dress and unrealistic behavior of the cosmopolitan in chapter 33.

When he came to write *Don Quixote*, Cervantes was
in the cells of the Holy Inquisition in La Mancha. He
alluded to the bitterness he felt about his captivity in
the opening lines of *Don Quixote*, but his literary situation was a precarious one. He needed to manage his
satire in a delicate way. For, according to Viardot, he
neither desired to mislead those who might miss his
subtle satire nor wanted to offend those few influential
readers who might detect the "bold criticisms" he had
smuggled into his book.[25] The implied solution to this
difficulty, and one that Melville probably would have
noted for himself, was to make his principal character
mad and therefore laughable and unreliable, though Cervantes himself, particularly in part 2 of his novel, might
speak through him. Cervantes imagined his knight-
errant in a "period between the extinction of ancient
and the rise of modern civilization," when the exploits
of knights-errant might be made to comment on the
customs of the age, much as Melville himself had made
the confidence man a vehicle for a satire on human gullibility and avarice and a taste for modern "improvements."
Additionally, Viardot observed, "Don Quixote was not
the first madman of his kind, the fictitious hero of La
Mancha had had living precursors, models of flesh and
blood."[26] This statement may have partly justified Melville's assertion, in fact, that original characters, Don
Quixote among them, cannot be "born" in the imagination.

Cervantes's original object of satire was a literary one.
He wished to attack those chivalric romances that had
misguided his country's youth, to attack that "hydra,"
as Viardot described it, which set common sense at a
distance. This, in part, seems to have been Melville's
intent as well. When one recalls the pointed satire of the
easy moral solutions dramatized in the popular literature of the times, especially of certain transcendentalist
writers, and Melville's specific criticism of a forced con-

sistency of character contained in the "best novels pro-
fessing to portray human nature," which are more apt to
mislead the "studious youth" than to guide him, it is evident that Melville's own satirical ambitions resembled
Cervantes's.[27] The Spanish author had hinted anonymously
in a pamphlet designed to publicize the first part of *Don
Quixote* that many of the characters in the book had
disguised reference to contemporary literary figures.
Given the fact that so many critics of *The Confidence-
Man* have argued, with varying degrees of persuasiveness, the presence of satirical portraits of several American figures, from Fanny Kemble to Bayard Taylor and
Joel Barlow, from Poe to Emerson and Thoreau, from
William Cullen Bryant to Theodore Parker and Horace
Greeley, it may well be that Cervantes provided Melville with a precedent for his own satire of literary figures.[28] The literary satire Melville worked into his book
is mostly to be found in the second half, the portion of
The Confidence-Man that appears to have been most
influenced by the example of Cervantes.

Still other resemblances further indicating the extent
to which Melville was influenced by Cervantes are suggested by Viardot's memoir. He may, for instance, have
decided to end his book with the ambiguous promise of
a sequel, partly in the hope that a popular reception of
his book would provide the demand for it, but also because he found his precedent in Cervantes. For, as Viardot
explained, it was fashionable in Cervantes's time to leave
such romances unfinished and in the midst of complicated adventures; and Cervantes himself had done so at
the conclusion of the first part of *Don Quixote,* though
at the time he had no intention of writing a second part.

The publication of the first and second parts of *Don
Quixote* was separated by some ten years, and Cervantes's attitude toward his subject and his title figure seems
to have changed during that interval. But that *Don Quixote* possesses two parts of a demonstrably different nature and emphasis was, for Viardot, not a defect but an
achievement: "The two portions of the work offer an

instance perfectly unique in the annals of literature, of a second part, being written on an after-thought, which not only equals, but surpasses the first. It is because the execution is not inferior, and the original ideas greater and more fertile—it is because the work addresses itself to all nations and all times—it is because it speaks the universal language of human nature."[29]

This shift, even transcendence, marked by the second part of *Don Quixote* is evident in several ways. Notably, there is a detectable change of attitude toward his main characters; Cervantes manifests a genuine affection for Don Quixote and Sancho Panza, argues Viardot, "and soon, in equal and well-regulated portions, he divides between them his judgement and his wit." As I will show, Melville betrays a similar change of attitude toward his main character, and at times chose to speak through him rather than to simply use him as a satirical vehicle. By developing and enlarging the qualities of Don Quixote and Sancho Panza, Cervantes sought to deliver a "critique of human nature generally," to survey types of humanity and expose their shortcomings by their encounters with his two main characters. A particular example of this shift of attitude observed by Viardot is signaled by the introduction of the character Samson Carasco, "an incredulous skeptic, who laughs at everything without restraint and without respect."[30] This description might serve as well for Melville's character Pitch, the Missouri bachelor, for Pitch is also an incredulous skeptic—one who rails against the trustworthiness of boys and yet agrees to hire one after his debate with the P.I.O. man; who afterward curses himself for his own gullibility and is puzzled by his own credulousness; and who finally regains his skeptical attitudes and parries with the confidence man in his final masquerade as Frank Goodman, the manifestation of the title figure that most resembles Don Quixote.

There are similarities too in Viardot's description of the methods Cervantes employed to put himself in a work that began as a simple though bitter satire. *Don*

Quixote was written, says Viardot, with too much wit to be comprehended by everyone, for "it was necessary to use some ingenuity, to put the emissaries of the holy office on a false scent":

> This will account for the caution observable in some instances, and we cannot too much admire the adroit management, the double meaning, the sly allusions, and the delicate irony so cleverly veiled, which Cervantes used to disguise to the inquisition, thoughts too boldly conceived, too insulting, and too profound to be openly and without reserve avowed.[31]

These are qualities of style that every sensitive reader of *The Confidence-Man* has detected for himself. And we have already noted how Melville smuggled into his narrative his own religious skepticism and personal cynicism by adapting the confidence man's masquerade in a way that paralleled Paul's types of the faithful. But, as we shall see, Melville found other ways to disguise his agnosticism, ways, in fact, that resemble those of Cervantes. For double entendre, sly allusion, and ambiguous irony so permeate *The Confidence-Man* that it remains one of his most perplexing books.

Yet another literary precedent Cervantes provided Melville was the former's tendency to put himself in his book by interpolating stories with direct, if private, reference to his own life. The "Story of the Morisco," of which Melville was reminded while off the coast of Algiers, has reference to the interpolated story of the Spanish captive in *Don Quixote*, which tells of Cervantes's own experience at the hands of his Moorish captors. As we shall see in the next chapter, the personal element in *The Confidence-Man* is mostly to be found in the interpolated chapters as well.

Finally, there is the example of the character Don Quixote himself. However removed this character may be from a swindler, Melville could nevertheless imagine a champion of charity and confidence who, however sinister his real purpose, might be taken for a quixotic simpleton in a corrupt age so terribly out of joint. For

Melville made his cosmopolitan quixotic in both the conventional and an imitative sense. Melville marked only the first sentence of the following passage from the Viardot introduction, but the whole passage deserves attention:

> Don Quixote is but the case of a man of diseased brain; his monomania is that of a good man who revolts at injustice, and who would exalt virtue. He indulges a day-dream of making himself the comforter of the afflicted, the champion of the weak, the terror of the proud and the wicked. On all other subjects he reasons admirably, he utters eloquent dissertations; he is fitter, as Sancho says, *rather to be a preacher than a knight-errant.*[32] (italics Viardot's)

Earlier, Melville had treated monomania of a rather different sort in the character of Ahab, but in the character of Frank Goodman he created a genial and vocal advocate of unqualified confidence, who at least on the surface appears to suffer from an equal, though less splenetic, obsession. The special quality of his obsession, coupled with his glad-handed eloquence, makes him something of an evangel of confidence aboard a ship of fools appropriately named the *Fidèle*, more interested in bargaining for a man's confidence than for his pocketbook.

Melville had written in *Pierre* that "No one great book must ever be separately regarded and permitted to domineer with its own uniqueness upon the creative mind; but that all existing great works must be federated in fancy."[33] Melville's reading of the Bible, Shakespeare, and Milton, as well as contemporary newspapers and magazines, served in one way or another to spur his own creative imagination, but his reading of *Don Quixote* seems to have influenced his treatment of the cosmopolitan more than the others and to have been "federated" in the most subtle and interesting ways. In sum, the complexity of the influence that Cervantes's novel appears to have had on Melville's creative imagination is to be found: (1) in the quality of impracticality he imposed on his confidence man in the character's final masquerade; (2) in his interest in Cervantes's narrator, Cid Hamet, who felt the compulsion to vary his sequential narrative by the interpolation of short stories; and (3) by the varieties of obsession Melville considered in his own interpolated stories, which he may well have considered varieties of quixotism.

The difference between Melville's confidence man in the role of Frank Goodman and Shakespeare's Autolycus is that Goodman, though he shares the other's sportiveness, gains nothing except the value of a single shave by his elaborate engagements in the confidence game. After accosting the misanthropic Missouri bachelor (whom he soon abandons), Goodman is himself accosted by Charlie Noble, another Mississippi operator. Later he is approached by a mystic, Mark Winsome (through whom he meets Winsome's disciple, Egbert). These characters, the peddler of a rhapsodical tract, and the barber are the contacts Goodman makes before the "increase in seriousness" of the final chapter. This in itself is suggestive of Don Quixote, whose three friends, a barber, a curate, and a bachelor, assume disguises and attempt to dissuade the knight from his madness. But, be that as it may, the important fact about the last half of the book is that the confidence man abandons his avariciousness and preaches the gospel of charity with decided zeal and apparent sincerity, becoming a sort of impractical knight-errant who attacks the ills of the world with his verbal lance.

The cosmopolitan's quixotic impulses are many. He tries to convert a misanthrope; he defends the noble red man against the claims of an Indian hater; he urges his idealism upon a "man of serviceable knowledge" (198), Mark Winsome; and he persuades the suspicious barber to remove his sign of No Trust. He appears, in short, as a defender of charity, friendship, and confidence who finds in any resistance to these virtues a new adventure.

It is true that the confidence man in his other roles also endorses an unquestioning confidence, but the cosmopolitan is its most ambitious partisan, and he is distinguished by certain Quixote-like characteristics. The

cosmopolitan's dress, like Don Quixote's but in a different way, is a "little out of the common" (131), and he
smokes a pipe with a porcelain bowl on which are painted
in miniature "linked crests and arms of interlinked nations" (132). Considering his creed of confidence, the
design on his pipe might easily serve the cosmopolitan
as a coat of arms. And, like Quixote, the cosmopolitan's
authority is apparently self-ordained; he too is a zealot
with a mission. The cosmopolitan admits as much to
the surly Pitch: "To you, an Ishmael, disguising in sportiveness my intent, I came ambassador from the human
race, charged with the assurance that for your mislike
they bore no answering grudge, but sought to conciliate
accord between you and them. Yet you take me not for
the honest envoy, but I know not what sort of unheard-of
spy" (138).

The cosmopolitan is indeed "charged with assurance."
In addressing Pitch, Goodman "cavalierly" crosses one
leg in front of the other and, when asked, casually confesses
his calling; he is

> "a cosmopolitan, a catholic man; who, being such, ties
> himself to no narrow tailor or teacher, but federates, in
> heart as in costume, something of the various gallantries of
> men under various suns. Oh, one roams not over the gallant
> globe in vain. Bred by it, is a fraternal and fusing feeling. No
> man is a stranger. You accost anybody. Warm and confiding,
> you wait not for measured advances. And though, indeed,
> mine, in this instance, have met with no very hilarious
> encouragement, yet the principle of a true citizen of the
> world is still to return good for ill.—My dear fellow, tell me
> how I can serve you." (132–33)

Quixote-like, the cosmopolitan claims to act according
to certain "gallant" principles and later admits that his
kind yearns after a "founded rule of content" and has no
use for the "dupes" or "impostors" who advocate soli-
tude, suicide, or the advancement of learning (135). Apparently he, like Don Quixote, likes the old ways.

Perhaps taking inspiration from Cervantes, Melville
littered the second half of *The Confidence-Man* with

conventional wisdom in the form of proverbs, stories, maxims, and fables. Don Quixote's madness stemmed from his reading books on knight-errantry. The knight's behavior is modeled after past gallantries, and he continually cites analogues in tales of knight-errantry that he believes justify his seemingly mad conduct. The knight's droll squire, Sancho Panza, on the other hand, is notorious for quoting perplexing and often irrelevant proverbs. Sancho's penchant for such folk wisdom is the constant complaint of Don Quixote, although the knight is himself guilty of uttering proverbs upon occasion.

Melville may have remembered Don Quixote as particularly given to proverbializing, however. In his poem about the figure, he characterized the mad knight as one who "Cites obsolete saws / of chivalry's laws."[34] And in *The Confidence-Man*, the cosmopolitan is particularly fond of proverbs that support his genial view of mankind. To illustrate, we need only give some of the more obvious examples:

> ". . . it is almost a proverb, that a man of humor, a man capable of a good loud laugh—seem how he may in other things—can hardly be a heartless scamp." (163)

> "But even if experience did not sanction the proverb, that a good laugher cannot be a bad man, I should yet feel bound in confidence to believe it, since it is a saying current among the people, and I doubt not originated among them, and hence *must* be true; for the voice of the people is the voice of truth." (163)

> "I once heard say, 'Better ripe than raw.'" (173)

But the acquaintances of the cosmopolitan also speak in proverbs, though, Quixote-like, Goodman denies the validity of saws that do not support his rosy view of life. Charlie Noble, for example, attempts to comment on the "advancing spirit of geniality":

> "To pursue the thought," said the other, "every blessing is attended with some evil, and—"
> "Stay," said the cosmopolitan, "that may be better let pass for a loose saying, than for hopeful doctrine."(176)

Similarly, Mark Winsome quotes a passage from Eccle-
siasticus in support of his doctrine of labels:

> "Hence that significant passage in Scripture, 'Who will
> pity the charmer that is bitten with a serpent?'"
> "*I* would pity him," said the cosmopolitan, a little blunt-
> ly, perhaps. (191)

And the barber also quotes from the Apocrypha in support of his distrust: "I recalled what the son of Sirach
says in the True Book: 'An enemy speaketh sweetly with
his lips;' and so I did what the son of Sirach advises in
such cases: 'I believed not his many words'" (236). The
statement that such advice is contained in Scripture
disturbs the cosmopolitan, and he hurries off toward the
cabin in which is kept the boat's Bible in an effort to
verify the barber's recollection (which is actually not of
the "True Book" but of the Apocrypha). Such proverbial
expressions of wisdom are frequently the subject of debate in the second half of the novel. Frank Goodman and
Charlie Noble, for example, argue the merits of Polonius's
maxims; and Charlie's eulogy of the press, as Nathalia
Wright has pointed out, is in imitation of certain passages from Proverbs 23:29–32.[35]
　　More important than these parallels, perhaps, is the
fact that Don Quixote is a well-meaning scamp. As Cervantes was no doubt aware, *Don Quixote* is a picaresque
novel without the rogue. Although Cervantes's knight
is thoroughly, sometimes absurdly virtuous, he is nevertheless an unwitting mischiefmaker, as much so as
Autolycus is a deliberate one. Quixote's "adventures"
typically result in havoc, whether it be in attacking a
windmill, releasing prisoners, or slaughtering sheep mistaken for soldiers. In his inability to distinguish appearance from reality, Don Quixote's folly becomes a kind of
roguery; Sancho Panza, in fact, though he loves his master, at one point confesses that he really does not know
whether Quixote is a "rogue" or a "dunce." Melville's
confidence man is also a mischiefmaker, and, at least in
his roles as mute and cosmopolitan, he naively makes

more mischief than profit. The mute's "innocent" preach-
ments for charity, for example, cause "some stares to
change into jeers, and some jeers into pushes, and some
pushes into punches" (6).[36]

It is clear that Melville provided his main character
with many of the same qualities that journalists had
attributed to the original confidence man. And at least
in the chapter entitled "Renewal of Old Acquaintance,"
the author had borrowed directly from the exploits of
the criminal who had prompted the creation of the term
confidence man. But in searching out the "significances" of this confidence man, Melville turned to the general condition of fraud and deceit of the time in order to
flesh out his novel and give it the dimension of social
satire. He fully exploited his knowledge of contemporary types of confidence men and confidence games and
put them to literary use. And he had found that the
schemes of confidence men might be made to comment
satirically on the practices of respected social types who,
in their inability to have confidence in their fellowmen,
were in effect confidence men themselves. Journalists
had discovered before Melville that the confidence man
could be successfully used as a vehicle for their satirical
thrusts, and to some extent they recognized that quality
as part of the swindler's "originality," but Melville used
this device with far greater ingenuity and subtlety than
any journalist had done.

In most of the roles he plays and in many of the confidence games he employs, Melville's central character is
anything but original, however. The deaf-and-dumb act
of the man in cream colors, the pretended deformity of
Black Guinea, the sales of towns not yet built, the miracle drugs peddled by the herb doctor, all these were familiar methods of fraud and deception. The masquerade
of the confidence man consists mainly of successive
appearances as rather conventional criminal types.

Moreover, his creation of a mysterious swindler who
could exchange personalities as easily as costumes seems

to have threatened to reduce Melville's story to a series of apparently unrelated episodes. Without his customary unifying device of an involved narrator, and with a rather incongruent character, Melville must have detected a certain formless quality in his novel. At any rate, his adoption of an ironic pattern suggested by St. Paul's description of the types of the faithful for the confidence man's masquerade provided at once an imaginative unity to his narrative and additional "significance" to his title character.

Whenever Melville may have discovered than an "original character" might be made to unify an otherwise fragmented story, he seems to have most fully avoided the conventional type of swindler in his confidence man's final masquerade as Frank Goodman. Through this character he achieved a quality of ironic ambiguity that raises his novel above the level of ordinary satire. And it is mostly in the character of Goodman, too, that Melville explored significances derived not only from life but from literature as well. His discovery of the unifying capacity of character may have attended his development of the literary significances of the cosmopolitan, and Melville may have found additional intellectual justification or even inspiration for this sort of approach to his material in Coleridge's essay on Hamlet. Melville had probably been familiar with the essay for some time, and it may have influenced his approach to the creation of Ahab.[37] In any event, the following passage fairly describes what Melville seems to have been attempting to do in *The Confidence-Man*, particularly in the second half:

> There is a great significancy in the names of Shakespeare's plays. In the Twelfth Night, Midsummer Night's Dream, As You Like It, and Winter's Tale, the total effect is produced by a co-ordination of the characters as in a wreath of flowers. But in Coriolanus, Lear, Romeo and Juliet, Hamlet, Othello, &c., the effect arises from the subordination of all to one, either as the prominent person, or the principal object.[38]

This approach is consistent with the creative method suggested by the Agatha letters and is a notion echoed in *The Confidence-Man* by Melville himself:

> For much the same reason that there is but one planet to one orbit, so can there be but one such original character to one work of invention. Two would conflict to chaos. (239)

In singling out Satan, Hamlet, and Don Quixote as examples of truly original characters, Melville, with varying degrees of subtlety and complexity, made literary use of the creations of Milton, Shakespeare, and Cervantes and modified the satiric implications of his use of the Bible. He believed that an original character such as Hamlet or Don Quixote is an extremely rare occurrence and that such a character might organize and enrich an otherwise episodic narrative. He also seems to have felt that his own original character, despite his incongruent nature, unified his work and saved it from chaos.

Nevertheless, Melville, like Cervantes, included much interpolated material in his book. Although a novel such as *Don Quixote*, which is dominated by the title character and which includes many interpolated stories, or a tragedy such as *Hamlet*, which is dominated by Hamlet and which includes a play within a play, might have provided Melville with the precedent for interpolating a variety of stories in his novel, we cannot properly investigate those stories through the character of the confidence man. In order to treat *The Confidence-Man* fully, however, it is essential to explore the interpolated material, for nearly one-quarter of the novel consists of these stories and the three chapters that contain speculations on the nature of literature. The interpolated material cannot be approached through the central character (who is necessarily offstage), however, but through the narrator himself, who seems to have taken even more of his cues from Hamlet and Don Quixote than the confidence man did.

George Caleb Bingham, *Persuasive Speaker*, 1853–1855.
The St. Louis Art Museum.

Chapter 5

The Personal Element

The confidence man dominates Melville's novel much as Hamlet dominates Shakespeare's play or Don Quixote Cervantes's novel: the action of the main narrative is subordinate to him, and he has the capacity to reveal the nature of all those with whom he comes in contact. In *Israel Potter,* as Leon Howard has observed, the author had used his title character "primarily as a connecting device for sketches of historical characters";[1] and he had remained fairly faithful to his promise to his publishers that there would be "very little reflective writing in it; nothing weighty."[2] The confidence man also serves as a connecting device for the various episodes of this later novel, but for Melville he was a good deal more besides, and surely no one would maintain that *The Confidence-Man* contains "nothing weighty." Rather than merely connecting random episodes, the confidence man brings them into sharp dramatic focus and provides an imaginative unity to the central narrative. Melville had found a splendid vehicle for social and religious satire in his rogue, but, as the previous chapter has indicated, the author had high literary ambitions for his character as well. Perhaps as a result of his concern for the creation of a truly original character, Melville's personal sentiments were muffled or controlled and found their way into his novel only obliquely. At any rate, the mode of the autobiographical romance, which characterized his earliest writing, and extensive commentary on the action of the story, present in both *Moby-Dick* and *Pierre,* are almost wholly absent in this book.

In the first six of his novels, Melville had created a fictional persona to narrate his story with whom he identified to some extent and through whom he might

comment directly on the events of his narrative. And in
Pierre, his first experiment in third-person narration,
the narrator had served as an active commentator on
and expositor of the thoughts and feelings of that novel's hero. But in *The Confidence-Man* the narrator func-
tions in a rather different way.

The narrator of this novel is typically detached from
the events he is describing and thoroughly ambiguous
and nonjudgmental about the motives and feelings of
the characters aboard the *Fidèle;* for the most part, he is
hidden behind the veil of "smoky" prose (239) consistent with the ambiguous nature of the novel. But along-
side the main narrative there also exist much interpolated material and digressive passages, and it is in this
portion of the book that Melville, rather than his narrator, gave voice to certain personal sentiments. This material is of three sorts. The first consists of the three
Fielding-like chapters that comment directly on the nature and merits of the narrative itself. The second consists of the five short stories, which are interpolated
into the narrative but, together, possess a certain unity
of their own. The third consists of discursive remarks
spoken by one or more of the characters, who sometimes speak in character and sometimes do not. Since
these discursive portions form much of the substance of
the book, an examination of them is as necessary as an
examination of the title character.

The three interpolated literary chapters (14, 33, and
44) have a certain though perhaps unintended unity because all three serve as apologies by the author for various shortcomings in his novel. Chapter 14 is an "apology for whatever may have seemed amiss or obscure in
the character of the merchant" (71). Chapter 33 answers
an imagined complaint about the previous "antics" of
the cosmopolitan. And chapter 44 seeks to show the
"impropriety" of the phrase *quite an original* as it is
applied to the cosmopolitan. In each instance, Melville

drops the role of detached narrator and comments, as author, directly on the merits of his book, and more particularly on the success of certain of his characters as fictional creations. But however eloquently he may enter into a defense of his creation, the defense is itself a tacit admission of his feeling that his book did not satisfy the creative ambitions he had for it.

In chapter 13, immediately preceding the first digression, the man in the traveling cap and the merchant consider the story of the unfortunate man, which the latter had just related. The man with the traveling cap chastises his companion for grieving over the fate of this unfortunate whose wife, Goneril, surely could not be so malicious as she was painted, or if she were, then how fortunate for her husband to be finally rid of her. The merchant's sympathetic grief is relieved by such considerations, and he is moved by his friend's overwhelming confidence in man and providence. To remove whatever misgivings may remain in the merchant, the confidence man orders champagne to "bubble" them away. However, for the merchant, the drink works the opposite of its intended effect, for it causes him to ponder the vanity of confidence and charity. His skeptical statements shock his companion. And it is this reversal of character in the merchant as it is revealed by his cynical remarks which provides, superficially at least, the occasion for the auctorial intrusion of chapter 14.

The merchant's discontent, out of character for one who previously had proved himself "so full of confidence," may disturb some readers, the now-intrusive author suggests. The "sensible" reader may demand consistency of character in fiction, but he also typically demands that "while to all fiction is allowed some play of invention, yet, fiction based on fact should never be contradictory to it; and is it not a fact, that, in real life, a consistent character is a *rara avis*?" (69). Caught upon the horns of this dilemma—the conflict between the consistency expected in fiction and the inconsistencies of

life to which it is expected to conform—the author ex-
cuses the writer who may create inconsistent characters on the grounds that Nature herself has made such
creations. He cites the flying squirrel as an animal "incongruous in its parts" and the caterpillar, which soon
becomes the butterfly, as "at variance with itself" (70).
And he notes that the duckbill beaver brought over from
Australia confounded certain English naturalists because
it defied their classifications.

Melville further argues that human nature consists of
murky waters, and that those authors who would represent it as "transparent" deceive themselves and their
readers. He further scorns the "sallies of ingenuity" that
certain "psychological novelists" have employed for the
purpose of revealing human nature on "fixed principles"
(71). Opposed to these novelists are the "more earnest
psychologists" who, "in the face of previous failures, still
cherish expectations with regard to some mode of infal-
libly discovering the heart of man" (71). Among this last
group of psychological novelists Melville may have included himself, for in *Pierre* he had attempted to explore
the "flowing river in the cave of man." And, though he applied no fixed principles in his investigation, he may
have felt *Pierre* both an artistic and psychological, as
well as a commercial, failure.

If Melville was referring to his earlier novel in this
passage and acknowledging its shortcomings, he may
also have been indicating his expectations for *The Confidence-Man*, yet sensing its failure to achieve them. The
comments of chapter 14 are much more instructive when
applied to the novel's title character than to a minor
character, the merchant, whose only inconsistency is a
brief, wine-induced reverie; and Melville may have had
his confidence man in mind when he wrote this chapter. It is the confidence man in his various roles who is
"incongruous" in his parts and "at variance" with himself. Melville may have recognized that his character,
incongruent in costume and mood, might baffle his read-

ers, but he was unwilling to accept the full burden of a reader's condemnation: "It must call for no small sagacity in a reader unerringly to discriminate in a novel between the inconsistencies of conception and those of life" (70).[3] The original confidence man had been, indeed, a riddle, involving many factual inconsistencies that Melville, in basing his fiction upon facts, felt bound to consider.

If chapter 14 is a defense of the author's right to pursue a strict realism even if it leads to the creation of superficially inconsistent characters, chapter 33 is a defense of the "fancy" that "shall envoke scenes different from those of the same old crowd round the custom-house counter . . . with characters unlike those of the same old acquaintances they meet in the same old way every day in the same old street" (182). Here he is evidently arguing for a different, less realistic approach to his character; and, appropriately enough, chapter 33 is an apology for the "antics" of the cosmopolitan. In most of his other disguises, the confidence man had appeared as a familiar type of rogue; but, as we have seen, Melville in "transforming" his title character derived the significance of the cosmopolitan more from literature than life. Instead of wishing for "sagacious" readers, as he had in chapter 14, Melville asked in chapter 33 for "tolerant" readers—"the more indulgent lovers of entertainment, before whom harlequin can never appear in a coat too parti-colored, or cut capers too fantastic" (183).

Chapter 33 is reminiscent of Hawthorne's claim in his preface to *The House of the Seven Gables* that the writer of romances has the right, and duty, to present the "truth of the human heart." Thus, he may feel free to "mingle the Marvelous" with realistic narrative.[4] In the chapter preceding 33, "Showing that the Age of Magic and Magicians Is Not Yet Over," the cosmopolitan has assumed the "air of a necromancer" in order to summon his companion from his uncharitable mood. Melville's subsequent commentary on this strange behavior reveals his feeling that tolerant readers "look not only for more entertainment, but, at bottom, even more reality than real life itself can show":

> Thus, though they want novelty, they want nature, too; but nature unfettered, exhilirated, in effect transformed. In this way of thinking, the people in a fiction, like the people in a play, must dress as nobody exactly dresses, talk as nobody exactly talks, act as nobody exactly acts. It is with fiction as with religion: it should present another world, and yet one to which we feel the tie. (183)

Taking his cues (as chapter 44 was to reveal) from Milton, Shakespeare, and Cervantes, Melville transformed his central character from a rather pedestrian criminal into something unique—his confidence man became rogue, fool, and quixotic idealist all in one, who might alternately swindle, ridicule, and inspire all whom he meets. Yet even with the cosmopolitan, though Melville was aiming at high literary accomplishment, he presumably anticipated failure and addressed his reader in advance with a request for "pardon" for a "well-meant endeavor" (183).

In chapter 44, we find the author once more apologizing for the failings of the cosmopolitan as an original character. It is clear from this chapter that the author wished to create a truly original character, but it is equally clear that he felt that the cosmopolitan, though certainly "striking," did not rival Hamlet, Don Quixote, or Milton's Satan. Though he had had much "good luck" in finding a prototype for his confidence man "in town," Melville's conception of his character apparently disappointed him. Thus, he finds the designation of the cosmopolitan as "quite an original" inappropriate—his character, he seems to have felt, was "almost, but not quite an original." The exuberance that had led him to compare Hawthorne favorably with Shakespeare in "Hawthorne and His 'Mosses'" does not appear in his appraisal of his own literary accomplishment in *The Confidence-Man*. But the author's acknowledgments of his novel's shortcomings do not seem to have proceeded from a lack of ambition. It is unlikely that he would have suggested the comparison of his character to those of Milton, Shakespeare, and Cervantes had he not felt a desire to emulate them.[5]

These chapters, in which Melville directly enters his book to comment on its merits, show that he was not a detached observer of the events of his novel. As Hennig Cohen has pointed out, Melville's talents "lay in the direction of extension, elaboration, involution, diversity, and digression," and in these interpolated chapters he had freely exercised those talents.[6] The restrictions he had placed on his main narrative by detached description of the adventures of a mysterious, protean figure had created a mystery that required interpolated commentary and explanation. Moreover, the personal element found in these three chapters is also evident, though in a different way, in the interpolated stories in the book.

The five interpolated stories in Melville's novel have attracted considerable critical attention, but critics have not observed the unifying theme that runs throughout them.[7] Nor has anyone remarked that the literary influences that contributed to the formation of the confidence man also exerted considerable influence on some of these stories and therefore give them an organic place in the book as a whole. These stories are successively those of "The Unfortunate Man" in chapter 12 and "A Soldier of Fortune" in chapter 19, which appear in the first half of the novel, and those of the Indian hater in chapter 27, the gentleman-madman in chapter 34, and China Aster in chapter 40, which appear in the second half. All of these stories have two things in common. First, they all deal in a somewhat ambiguous way with some form of real or pretended madness from a point of view related to Melville's conception of Cervantes's mad knight, Don Quixote, as he expressed it in a poem on "The Rusty Man." Second, they all are related to Hamlet's "To be or not to be" soliloquy.

The extensive use of interpolated stories was new to Melville's art.[8] In part, it probably derived from his re-

cent experience as a contributor to magazines. He had
been cultivating the art of the short story for the past
three years, and it may have become fairly easy for him.
The idea of interpolating them within the framework of
a longer story, however, probably came from his current
interest in *Don Quixote*. Melville's annotations in his
copy of this novel reveal a special interest in the supposed narrator of Cervantes's book, Cid Hamet, who is
usually as unobtrusive as Melville's own narrator. In the
back flyleaf of the second volume of his copy, Melville
had kept a list of references to the Arabic narrator and
may have paid particular attention to the supposed author's defense of digression at the beginning of chapter
44 in part 2 of the novel.[9] That chapter records Cid
Hamet's complaints about the limitations of his story
and the restraints placed on his genius, since he felt he
could not simply tell the story of his mad knight and, at
the same time, "launch out into episodes and digres-
sions of more weight and entertainment."[10] Thus, in
order to relieve himself of this "insupportable toil," he
worked minor tales into his major narrative. This is
precisely what Melville did in *The Confidence-Man*.

All five stories are tales of ambiguous "madness" of
the sort Melville found in Cervantes's Knight of the
Woeful Countenance and entitled "The Rusty Man /
(By a Timid One)":[11]

> In La Mancha he mopeth,
>   With beard thin and dusty;
> He doteth and mopeth
>   In library fusty—
> 'Mong his old folios gropeth:
>   Cites obsolete saws
>   Of chivalry's laws—
>   *Be the wronged one's knight:*
>   Die, but do right.
> So he rusts and musts,
> While each grocer green
> Thriveth apace with the fulsome face
> Of a fool serene.

In contrast to the high-minded and enthusiastic idealism of Don Quixote, it is, in Melville's day, the complacent greengrocer who prospers. Trade has made chivalry
out of date; the serene face goes with insincerity and
baseness, while the idealist wears a woeful countenance
as he mopes over the musty maxims of justice and charity and for that reason is considered mad. All of the
central characters in Melville's five stories are "mad" in
a similarly ambiguous way.

The first interpolated story, "The Story of the Unfortunate Man," had followed a rather devious course before it finally entered the book in chapter 12. It was first
told by the man with the weed to the merchant, authen-
ticated and to some extent amplified by the man in gray,
and then retold by the merchant to the man in the traveling cap. Finally, the narrator, feeling that the merchant
could do "better justice to the man than the story" (59),
undertakes to tell the story to the reader in words other
than the merchant's.

Its hero is what Melville had called in *Pierre* a "fool of
virtue"; his troubles were caused not so much by his
wife's behavior as his own reactions to it. The unfortunate man believes his wife guilty of certain "mysterious
touchings" and of playing the "maternal hypocrite" (62-63)
with their daughter. He decides to take his complaints
to the law, which he deems the most Christian course
since the courts would not be "at variance with the
truth of the matter" (63). The courts sided with Goneril,
of course; and, when it appeared that the charges of
insanity brought against her by the unfortunate man
might actually recoil upon him, he fled to the West.
Ever true to his foolish notions of virtue, the unfortunate man, on learning through the newspapers of the
death of Goneril, wears a weed in his hat, for he felt it
but "proper to comply with the prescribed form of mourning in such cases" (63).

The unfortunate man's quixotic behavior is at once
admirable and foolish, but the world at large would judge
him mad. He had attempted to get his wife convicted of
"mental derangement" but found that the sentiments

of society and the court sided with Goneril. And it is he, not she, who became liable to "be permanently committed for a lunatic" (63) because of his "self-respect" and "Christian charity towards Goneril" (62). There is a special irony in this story because it not only serves to characterize the unfortunate man as a fool of virtue, but is told to the sympathetic Mr. Roberts, who proves himself a fool by giving a "large bill" out of pity to the man with the weed.

The story of "A Soldier of Fortune" in chapter 19 (told by himself) also deals with a kind of behavior that a complacent world might deem "mad." It tells of Thomas Fry, once known as Happy Tom, whose misfortune was to be witness to a murder. He is held in the Tombs because he has no friends to go bail for him, while the murderer, who does, goes free and is eventually acquitted. His damp cell in the Tombs makes a cripple of Fry before he is finally free to go, but by that time the only place he can go is the Corporation Hospital. After three years upon his iron bed, he decides to leave and upon departure receives five silver dollars and a pair of crutches for his pains.

The soldier of fortune had been as impractically "mad" as Don Quixote in his attempt to be an honest witness despite the overbearing injustice of his confinement. And the crippling outcome of his honesty seems to have developed in him a comparably odd behavior, for in the presence of the herb doctor he is given to fits of "strangely startling" laughter coupled with spontaneous and sarcastic outbursts against "free Ameriky" (98). His sardonic attitude, along with necessity, has in fact caused him to practice his own special and cynical brand of confidence game.

A third story, comparable to these in succinctness and tone, is told by Frank Goodman in the second half of the book. "The Story of the Gentleman-Madman" is, as Leon Howard has observed, "a retelling of the story of Jimmy Rose" (which Melville published in *Harper's* in

November 1855 while still working on *The Confidence-Man*) "with the hero of the new version merely affecting a misanthropic attitude out of sensitivity while he actually preserved his courage, made a new fortune, and reassumed his place in society as though nothing had happened."[12] This story is particularly interesting because its hero, though called a "madman," behaves in a way that seems exceptionally sane. Although Charlemont, the hero of Melville's new story, had shown signs of a "mind suddenly thrown from its balance" shortly before his bankruptcy, he did not return to his old haunts as an object of charity, as did Jimmy Rose, but seemed to display his previous assurance—although he did reveal a secret bitterness to one friend who asked him to explain "the enigma of his life." This revelation persuades the friend that "some taint of Charlemont's old malady survived, and it was not well for friends to touch one dangerous string" (186).

The story of Charlemont also is of particular interest because of its personal implications. The story is immediately preceded by one of the digressive chapters on literature in which the author remarks that "so precious to man is the approbation of his kind, that to rest, though but under an imaginary censure applied to but a work of imagination, is no easy thing" (183). Hershel Parker, in a note on this passage in the Norton edition of *The Confidence-Man*, suggests that it is "an oblique comment on the critical reception of some of Melville's earlier books," especially *Pierre*, "the censure of which was anything but imaginary."[13] But the reference may well go back to *Mardi*, for Melville, like Charlemont, was in his twenty-ninth year when he published that unsuccessful work of imagination and was "gazetted" into literary bankruptcy. Like Charlemont, Melville recouped his fortunes by rapidly producing *Redburn* and *White-Jacket* the following year. The experience was repeated, of course, with the failure of *Pierre* and his subsequent turn to magazine writing; but Melville may have been justifying his own motives in writing both *Moby-Dick* and *Pierre*, as well as his reconciliation to magazine writing, when he had Charlemont say:

> If ever, in days to come, you shall see ruin at hand, and, thinking you understand mankind, shall tremble for your friendships, and tremble for your pride; and, partly through love for the one and fear for the other, shall resolve to be beforehand with the world, and save it from a sin by prospectively taking that sin to yourself, then will you do as one I now dream of once did, and like him will you suffer; but how fortunate and how grateful should you be, if like him, after all that had happened, you could be a little happy again. (185–86)

The sort of idealism practiced by the unfortunate man, once practiced and now despised by the soldier, and concealed by Charlemont was of the sort Melville admired and (if we can trust the personal implications of the last story) found in himself. It was quixotic and impractical not because it was madness but because it was out of date.

"The Story of the Gentleman-Madman" is the only one told by the confidence man himself, and the personal quality found in it suggests the interesting possibility that Melville himself may have identified, at least at times, with his central character after he had begun to masquerade as Frank Goodman. At any rate, there is surely some significance in the fact that each of the two remaining stories was told by a character whom the cosmopolitan calls "Charlie"—the story of the Indian hater by Charles Arnold Noble, who asks to be called by that nickname, and the story of China Aster by Mark Winsome's practical disciple, Egbert, who willingly accepts the designation at the cosmopolitan's suggestion. In mid-nineteenth-century slang a "Charlie" was a particular type of confidence man sometimes known as a "thimble-rigger," a sleight-of-hand artist whose special confidence game was to have his victim guess which of three rapidly manipulated thimbles concealed a pea that he had actually removed from the table. In employing the term, Melville meant to suggest the hypocrisy of both Noble and Egbert. But the term also is indicative of the verbal sleight of hand the stories these men tell might contain; any tale told by a "Charlie" should have in it more than meets the eye.

The protagonist in each of these last two stories is also mad in his way, although their madness is not the chivalric sort but the obsessive "Quixotism" Melville would later attribute to the Zionist Deacon Dickson when he met him in the Holy Land. On one hand, China Aster, like the unfortunate man, is foolishly virtuous and idealistic. On the other, Colonel Moredock, like the soldier of fortune after his sufferings, is cynical and malicious. Yet in these tales Melville pursued the themes set forth in the earlier stories to further extremes and gave them greater substance. The grief of the unfortunate man is as pathetic and conventional as the weed he wears to symbolize it, but China Aster's obsessive dedication to virtue approaches tragedy. And, in contrast to the petty chicaneries and rather ordinary cynicism of the soldier of fortune, Colonel Moredock is a "good hater"—a genuine zealot devoting his life to revenge.

The last story in the book, "The Story of China Aster," is especially bitter. Both Elizabeth Foster and Leon Howard have suggested that the tale may have been written earlier than its place in the narrative suggests, and Howard says that it is the only one of the short stories "out of harmony with its place in the book."[14] A more recent study of this story by James Barbour and Robert Sattelmeyer, however, argues persuasively that Melville may have been consciously satirizing the kind of moral tale that formed the greater portion of the library of the *Charles and Henry*, on which Melville had served for three inactive months but had particular reference to the homiletic tales found in a New England periodical entitled, appropriately enough, the *China Aster*, which was published irregularly from 1845 to 1851.[15]

Melville's story of an honest candlemaker's ruin by

his acceptance of a loan forced upon him by a friend was
a brutal satire of Victorian moralizing; and its meaning
was made explicit by the inscription China Aster had
himself composed for his gravestone:

'HERE LIE
THE REMAINS OF
CHINA ASTER THE CANDLE-MAKER,
WHOSE CAREER
WAS AN EXAMPLE OF
THE TRUTH OF SCRIPTURE, AS FOUND
IN THE
SOBER PHILOSOPHY
OF
SOLOMON THE WISE;
FOR HE WAS RUINED BY
ALLOWING HIMSELF TO BE PERSUADED,
AGAINST HIS BETTER SENSE,
INTO THE FREE INDULGENCE OF CONFIDENCE,
AND
AN ARDENTLY BRIGHT VIEW OF LIFE,
TO THE EXCLUSION
OF
THAT COUNSEL WHICH COMES BY HEEDING
THE
OPPOSITE VIEW.' (219)

This tale, however, displays the same ambiguity found
in the others by making China Aster's madness undefinable. The epitaph, the narrator tells us, was probably
written "in one of those disconsolate hours, attended
with more or less mental aberration, perhaps, so frequent with him for some months prior to his end" (218).
But is the narrator to be trusted? The sort of moralist
Melville was satirizing might call China Aster mad, but
the perceptive reader may have been expected to see
him as a "fool of virtue" who had come to his senses.

If China Aster, like Pierre, indulged his conscience in
an ardently bright view of life "against his better sense,"
as his epitaph had suggested, Colonel Moredock, the In-

dian hater, like Captain Ahab, was indulging in a destructive obsession or ardently dark view. Like the other stories, the tale of the Indian hater has as its protagonist one who suffers from a special kind of madness. In constructing the other stories, Melville may have taken his cue from Cervantes's novel in a rather general way, but in the story of Moredock the influence is clear and specific.

The story of the Indian hater is particularly ambiguous in its implications because it is told by the Mississippi operator, Charlie Noble, and is commented on by the confidence man in his role as Frank Goodman, who sometimes speaks, as we shall see, for Herman Melville. Although it is a true story—Melville derived it from Judge James T. Hall's *Sketches of History, Life, and Manners in the West* (1835)—the cosmopolitan is incredulous: "As for this Indian-hating in general, I can only say of it what Dr. Johnson said of the alleged Lisbon earthquake: 'Sir, I don't believe it' " (157). Goodman concedes, however, that if such a man as Moredock ever existed, then his "lone campaigns are fabulous as Hercules' " (156). Ironically, it is the extraordinary cosmopolitan who represents the ordinary world when he calls the colonel a madman: "God bless me; hate Indians? Surely, the late Colonel Moredock must have wandered in his mind" (140). Whether real or not, Moredock's madness parallels that of Cervantes's mad knight.

Moredock, though considered no Indian hater *"par excellence,"* is presented as an adequate representation of the particular breed of backwoodsman who, according to Charlie Noble, ought to be compared to such past heroes as "Moses in the Exodus, or the Emperor Julian in Gaul" (145). But, like Don Quixote, the Indian hater derives his passion from the authorities of a past age:

> Accordingly, if in youth the backwoodsman incline to knowledge, as is generally the case, he hears little from his schoolmasters, the old chroniclers of the forest, but histories of Indian lying, Indian theft, Indian double-dealing, Indian fraud and perfidy, Indian want of conscience, Indian blood-

thirstiness, Indian diabolism—histories which, though of wild woods, are almost as full of things unangelic as the Newgate Calendar or the Annals of Europe. In these Indian narratives and traditions the lad is thoroughly grounded. (146)

These "forest histories," of which the story of the Wrights and Weavers is an example, inspire the Indian hater to make a vow and commit himself to knightlike austerity:

An intenser Hannibal, he makes a vow, the hate of which is a vortex from whose suction scarce the remotest chip of the guilty race may reasonably feel secure. Next, he declares himself and settles his temporal affairs. With the solemnity of a Spaniard turned monk, he takes leave of his kin; or rather, these leave-takings have something of the still more impressive finality of death-bed adieus. Last, he commits himself to the forest primeval; there, so long as life shall be his, to act upon a calm, cloistered scheme of strategical, implacable, and lonesome vengeance. (149–50)

Like the Quixote of Melville's poem, the Indian hater is also something of an anachronism, for Charlie Noble informs us that "Indian rapine having mostly ceased through regions where it once prevailed, the philanthropist is surprised that Indian-hating has not in like degree ceased with it" (144).

These remarks, which occur in chapter 26, serve as an "introduction" (152) to the story of Moredock himself. The young Moredock's immediate attempt to avenge the injury done him gradually becomes a way of life. Although among friends and neighbors he was a "moccasined gentleman, admired and loved" (154), he passed over the rewards that such admiration might accrue (including the possibility of becoming governor), preferring the hard life of a committed Indian hater. To be a consistent Indian hater, Nobel tells us, "involves the renunciation of ambition, with its objects—the pomps and glories of the world; . . . Indian-hating, whatever may be thought of it in other respects, may be regarded as not wholly without the efficacy of a devout sentiment" (155).

At the conclusion of "The Story of China Aster," the cosmopolitan objects to Egbert's story as an attempt to destroy his confidence. Egbert replies that the "best man, as the worst, is subject to all mortal contingencies. He may travel, he may marry, he may join the Come-Outers, or some equally untoward school or sect, not to speak of other things that more or less tend to new-cast the character" (222). If Melville himself "new-cast" his old "mad" characters, Ahab and Pierre, in rather different situations, he did not reach decidedly different conclusions about them. He not only improved Judge Hall's prose in his redaction, but he also transformed Moredock into a vengeful knight and his peculiar passion into a "holy sentiment," though perhaps a mad one. And, in his story meant to recall the juvenile journal the *China Aster*, he had introduced into the ordinarily jejune moral tale certain ambiguities that made the plight of a "fool of virtue" infinitely more complex than did the stories common to such journals.

At any rate, it is clear that Melville did not share Egbert's conviction that men are but the pawns of circumstance. At the conclusion of chapter 14, Melville had argued that a "true map" of human nature, like a map of Boston, may reveal many devious "twistings," and he had elaborated upon this analogy: "Nor, to this comparison, can it be an adequate objection, that the twistings of the town are always the same, and those of human nature subject to variation. The grand points of human nature are the same to-day as they were a thousand years ago. The only variability in them is in expression, not in feature" (71). The imaginative unity that the author found in these five very different sets of circumstances resulted in a kind of dramatic resolution that the complacent world at large would call madness.

Perhaps the thematic coherence Melville achieved in these stories by suggesting the possible madness of their respective heroes was enriched by certain suggestions taken from another hero with a woeful countenance who was reputed mad—Hamlet, to whom Melville compared his own character although, as we have seen, that character's Shakespearean qualities were derived mostly from Autolycus. The five stories may have been Melville's response, though certainly not an answer, to questions posed in Hamlet's "To be, or not to be" soliloquy. In any case, it is interesting to note that the stories seem to share parallels with certain passages in that speech.

The story of the unfortunate man is a tale of the "pangs of despis'd love," with an additional Shakespearean implication in the name of his wife, Goneril. The soldier of fortune is one who has suffered from the "insolence of office" and the "law's delay." The story of Charlemont is one of a reaction to "contumely." And, taken together, the stories of China Aster and Colonel Moredock make it an even question whether it is

> nobler in the mind to suffer
> The slings and arrows of outrageous fortune
> Or to take arms against a sea of troubles
> And by opposing end them.

Certainly China Aster is one who suffers "the spurns / That patient merit of th' unworthy takes"; and Colonel Moredock's immediate reaction to the news of his mother's death is to take arms against her murderers.

Whether or not the relationship of *Don Quixote* and *Hamlet* to the five stories was a germinal one, it is clear that Melville took many of his cues in writing them from their authors. The level of ambiguity attained by both Cervantes and Shakespeare had been achieved in part by the same means Melville used in his novel. Cervantes heightened the reader's interest in his mad knight by revealing in him an uncommon lucidity and sanity at times; and the "crafty madness" of which Hamlet is suspected makes him all the more enigmatic. By hinting that the cosmopolitan and the protagonists of the five tales were possibly mad, Melville had deepened the significance of his novel as a whole. For, as we shall see in the final chapter, the theme of madness is directly related to the larger question of charity and confidence, with which *The Confidence-Man* is primarily concerned.

But if Melville found it convenient to deal with his personal preoccupation with the subject of madness and his own literary career in these interpolated stories, he also scattered throughout the novel discursive comments attributed to one character or another that seem to bear little relation to the story itself. And here too we find a personal element in the book.

For the most part, the frequent discursive conversations in *The Confidence-Man* are couched in the language of hyperbole, and the author's relationship to the topics under discussion is generally difficult to determine. Certainly Melville did not advocate the blind confidence that his title character so often advocates; but, despite his sardonic attitude, it is equally doubtful that he shared the cynicism of the Missouri bachelor, for example, whose distrust of boy servants and faith in the machine lead him to conclude that the working man will soon be a "superseded fossil" (117). Nevertheless, there are moments when Melville apparently gives voice to his personal sentiments through his characters. For example, Charlie Noble's contempt for Polonius's "false, fatal, and calumnious" (170) advice to Laertes is probably more representative of Melville's own feelings than is Pitch's attitude toward nature: "I don't deny but your clover is sweet, and your dandelions don't roar; but whose hailstones smashed my windows?" (109). This cynicism is consistent with Pitch's character, but nothing has prepared us for Charlie's remarks. Noble's heated opinions on such a literary subject are not in keeping with his feigned congeniality, nor would they seem to work to his advantage in his attempt to dupe the cosmopolitan. Rather, it was probably Melville himself who rejected the trite, "green grocer" wisdom of Polonius.

The practice of speaking through his own creations was not new to Melville. He had done it in *Mardi*, particularly in the colloquies of King Media and his counselors, Babbalanja, Mohi, and Yoomy. However, though Melville might speak through any of those characters, the excesses of thought of which some of the counselors, particularly Yoomy, were guilty, and which did not represent the author's personal views, were tempered by the common sense of Media. In *The Confidence-Man*, however, there is no figure equivalent to Media. Instead, the characters aboard the *Fidèle* generally are subject to those "queer, unaccountable caprices" of the "natural heart" (68). But there are times when certain characters come to their senses, much as Charlemont or China Aster do in their respective stories. Pitch does so when he curses himself for his foolish behavior with the P.I.O. man. And the barber, after his encounter with the cosmopolitan, is "restored to his self-possession and senses" (237), and he replaces his No Trust sign and tears up the agreement between the cosmopolitan and himself that bound him to give credit to his customers.

Something of this same sort of lapse into sanity is observable in the behavior of the merchant just previous to the discussion of inconsistency of character in chapter 14. The merchant, who had shown himself to be most charitable and sensitive, falls into meditation over the plight of the unfortunate man while sipping his wine. After some thought, he breaks the silence:

> Ah, wine is good, and confidence is good; but can wine or confidence percolate down through all the stony strata of hard considerations, and drop warmly and ruddily into the cold cave of truth? Truth will *not* be comforted. Led by dear charity, lured by sweet hope, fond fancy essays this feat; but in vain; mere dreams and ideals, they explode in your hand, leaving naught but the scorching behind! (67)

The confidence man is shocked by this outburst and attributes it to the effect of the champagne on the brain of the normally confident merchant. But the merchant, though unable to account for his change of sentiment, does not believe it due to a muddling of the brain: "If anything, the wine had acted upon it something like the white of egg in coffee, clarifying and brightening" (68).

Though the narrator characterizes the merchant's remarks as "mad disclosures" (68), it is clear from what we have said earlier that, though the world at large might find them mad, Melville meant to suggest that these were the sentiments of one who had suddenly come to his senses. In a novel that takes as its theme the Christian virtues of faith, hope, and charity (those qualities to which the confidence man consistently appeals), this is a particularly significant revelation of Melville's own probable feelings. However, as he had done with the interpolated stories, the author neutralized and made ambiguous those irreverent passages by suggesting the possible madness of their speaker.

Although Melville expressed his personal views through many different characters, he most often spoke through the confidence man in his role as the cosmopolitan. The possible personal implications of the story of Charlemont, which is told by the cosmopolitan, suggest that Melville at times identified with this character. At any rate, Frank Goodman's estimation of Shakespeare seems to reflect the author's personal feelings:

> ". . . to confess, in reading Shakespeare in my closet, struck by some passage, I have laid down the volume, and said: 'This Shakespeare is a queer man.' At times seeming irresponsible, he does not always seem reliable. There appears to be a certain—what shall I call it?—hidden sun, say, about him, at once enlightening and mystifying. Now, I should be afraid to say what I have sometimes thought that hidden sun might be." (171–72)

And, when asked by Charlie Noble whether that hidden sun might be the "true light," Goodman replies:

> "I would prefer to decline answering a categorical question there. Shakespeare has got to be a kind of deity. Prudent minds, having certain latent thoughts concerning him, will reserve them in a condition of lasting probation. Still, as touching avowable speculations, we are permitted a tether." (172)

In Melville's own estimation, his acquaintance with the "divine William" had marked an epoch in his life.[16]

Nevertheless, in his essay on "Hawthorne and His 'Mosses,'" he had argued against the notion that Shakespeare is "unapproachable."[17] Those sentiments are echoed in the words of Frank Goodman, and no doubt the subsequent inquiry into the puzzling character of Autolycus also represents the author's personal views.

Apparently Melville also found the cosmopolitan an adequate spokesman for his own objections to transcendentalist thought, for it is Frank Goodman who expresses contempt for the "moonshiny" and "inhuman" philosophy of Mark Winsome. Goodman's objections to this philosophy throughout the interview with both Winsome and Egbert are very close to feelings Melville expressed about Emerson in letters and in annotations to certain passages in books by or about the man.[18]

Elizabeth Foster, who argues that Winsome and Egbert represent the theoretical and practical aspects of Emerson's thought respectively, has fully documented Melville's reaction to the transcendentalist and has identified interesting parallels between Melville's portraits of his transcendentalist characters and certain notions expressed in Emerson's writings.[19] It is interesting to note that Foster, though she believes the confidence man to be an allegorical representative of the Devil, argues that in this encounter Melville intended the reader to wholly sympathize with the cosmopolitan: "So inhuman have Winsome and Egbert shown themselves that the cosmopolitan begins to look like the true champion of magnanimity and benevolence after all. Melville's quiet reminder, at the end of the scene with Egbert, that the cosmopolitan is playing a role is hardly clear or strong enough to dethrone him now in the reader's sympathy."[20] She further argues that the cosmopolitan's eloquence in this episode suggests a depth of conviction and feeling that "came from his [Melville's] own heart."

In his satirical treatment of Mark Winsome and Egbert, Melville surely spoke through his central character. And the personal sentiments he had expressed toward these transcendentalists indicate that he was probably

speaking from the heart when he had the cosmopolitan
utter somewhat sympathetic criticisms of the rhapsodical beggar who interrupts the conversation between
Winsome and Goodman.

Harrison Hayford has persuasively argued that this
figure is the "type-exponent" of Edgar Allan Poe.[21] Moreover, he observes that the context of Melville's satire
demanded that this character reject a brand of transcen-
dentalism that was not a commercial success, for it is
Winsome, despite his mysticism, who keeps his eye on
the "main chance." Thus, the appearance of this "crazy
beggar" enabled Melville to expose the cold practicality
of Winsome (who refuses to purchase a copy of the poeti-
cal tract from the beggar) as well as to make gentler fun
of another type of transcendentalist. Through the words
and actions of the cosmopolitan, it becomes clear that
Melville was much more sympathetic toward the Poe-
like rhapsodist than toward the Emerson-like Winsome.

The cosmopolitan purchases a copy of the tract and,
after the departure of the salesman, chastises Winsome
for refusing him: "Come, now, . . . you ought to have
sympathized with that man; tell me, did you feel no
fellow-feeling? Look at this tract here, quite in the transcendental vein" (195). Winsome replies that he never pa-
tronizes "scoundrels" and that this beggar was such a
man because he had perceived in him a "damning peep
of sense—damning, I say; for sense in a seeming madman is scoundrelism" (195). Winsome's criticisms recoil upon him, however, when the cosmopolitan replies,
"As for his adroitly playing the madman, invidious critics might object the same to some one or two strolling
magi of these days" (195).

As Hayford has perceptively remarked, it is precisely
a "peep of sense" that damns Winsome himself: "The
implication is that Winsome-Emerson only plays at his
own madness, to get money; he has sense enough not to
act on his philosophy in any way damaging to health,
wealth, common sense, or clean clothes."[22] In light of
the pervasive theme of madness in Melville's book, how-

ever, Hayford's observation is still more provocative. Winsome, Egbert, and to a lesser extent the rhapsodist are worldly opposites to the quixotism that Melville admired. Unlike Charlemont, whose "madness" was the result of an attempt to be "beforehand" with the world, these transcendentalists only pretend to madness in order to line their pockets. Rather than high-minded idealists, they are literary "green grocers"—shrewd, deceptive, complacent—who cater to the fancies of the contemporary public.

The "shrewdness and mythiness" (189) in Melville's Mark Winsome identify the transcendentalist as a humbug. Winsome appears "a kind of cross between a Yankee peddler and Tartar priest, though it seemed as if, at a pinch, the first would not in all probability play second fiddle to the last" (189). Like a more conventional confidence man, this mystic plays the public for dupes by appearing inspired and idealistic. And the pretended madness of Winsome provides yet another parallel to the episodes that deal with Winsome and Egbert and the more clearly identified swindler, Charlie Noble. For Noble, aware that the cosmopolitan himself seeks a loan, pretends drunkenness and curses that "elixir of logwood" for shortening their congenial interview. Goodman replies, "you are losing your mind" to talk so of mild wine, but the "madness" of Noble, like that of Winsome, is only a pose designed to insure his own best interests.

If indeed the story of the gentleman-madman has personal reference to Melville's own literary career, there is a special bitterness in his characterization of this transcendentalist as an impostor of madness. Melville himself had often enough been accused of madness by reviewers and presumably deeply resented the imputation.[23] Though he might easily have profited from his own reputation as the sailor-adventurer and the man who lived among cannibals and continued to write popular autobiographical romances, he had declined to do so; and he disdained the title of "the author of 'Typee' and 'Omoo.'" Rather, in a more daring spirit, he had explored uncharted waters in books like *Mardi, Moby-Dick,* and *Pierre.* Certainly the author of these books had not reaped huge profits from them; yet he seems to have felt that certain "scoundrel" writers had capitalized on a contrived madness. In this sense, Melville's satire of the transcendentalists is not merely intellectual; it also expressed a personal attitude toward his own literary fortunes and the fortunes of others.

George Caleb Bingham, *Substantial Citizen*, 1847.
Nelson Gallery—Atkins Museum (Nelson Fund).

Chapter 6

Ignis Fatuus:
Melville's Problem of Belief

This study began with the hypothesis that an adequate understanding of the significance of the central character would provide a clear picture of what Melville was trying to do in his book. That such a character existed despite the puzzling effectiveness of his various disguises has been demonstrated. Appearing first in the role of a mute apostle of charity, he dominated the book from beginning to end as he masqueraded in the first half as Black Guinea, John Ringman, the man in gray, the man with the traveling cap, the herb doctor, the P.I.O man, and, finally, in his last long masquerade as the cosmopolitan. As the mute, the confidence man's actions, in contrast to the businesslike ones of the barber, established the theme of the book, and their two signs, Charity Never Faileth and No Trust, dramatized the extremes of faith and faithlessness with which Melville was to deal throughout his narrative.[1]

This central character never achieved the unity and firmness normally expected of a character in fiction, nor did Melville intend that he should. On the contrary, in the penultimate chapter of his book Melville described the type of character he was trying to create as being essentially "like a revolving Drummond light, raying away from itself all round it—everything is lit by it, everything starts up to it" (239). Melville's interest in his central character was in his capacity to reveal the inner natures of those with whom he came in contact, not in him as a fictional personality. This mysterious impostor was, in effect, a satirical vehicle through whom Melville might ridicule a society characterized, on the

131

one hand, by the prevalence of dishonesty and gullibility and, on the other, by coldness and suspicion.

The first half of *The Confidence-Man* satirizes those passengers whose gullibility leads them to donate to false charities, invest in sham stocks, and purchase quack medicines. But the second half of this double-edged satire ridicules those who refuse to have confidence, including the misanthropic "boon companion," Charlie Noble, and the high-minded but unfeeling transcendentalists, Mark Winsome and Egbert. This shift in the object of Melville's satire represents a change of heart on the part of the author. Like the writer quoted by Evert Duyckinck in the *Literary World,* he came to believe that the man who is *"always* on his guard, *always* proof against appeal . . . is far gone, in our opinion, towards being himself a hardened villain."

But Melville did not use his character as an illuminator of his surroundings and nothing more. He was based, after all, on a real original whose discovery "in town" had provided Melville with a striking new phrase to use for the title of his book and in whom Melville found certain "significances," which he developed for their own sake. The most private and therefore most obscure of these are the religious significances. There is no question that the book demonstrates Melville's skepticism about the practical value of such Christian virtues as faith, hope, and charity; and the parallelism between the confidence man's roles and those of the members of the primitive Christian church to whom St. Paul attributed special "gifts" suggests that the character was intended to be in part a satire on "the faithful," and perhaps even a sardonic commentary on Christianity itself.

The precise depth of Melville's antireligious feelings when he wrote this book is impossible to determine, although they evidently ran deep. As Elizabeth Foster has shown in her study of the revisions of chapter 14, Melville toned down his agnosticism considerably; his method of revision, she asserts, had as its aim a "hush-

ing of the voice," the "meticulous moderation of thought."[2]
Nevertheless, despite the softening of its antireligious
sentiments, Newton Arvin has seen *The Confidence-
Man* as "one of the most completely *infidel* books ever
written by an American; one of the most completely
nihilistic morally and metaphysically."[3] There is no gain-
saying the bitter strain in the book, dark in its implications and, in many ways, cynical of both man and God.
But the blackness is not total.

It is relieved by the literary significances. Some of
these, especially the parallels with Milton's Satan, rein-
force the antireligious suggestiveness, because Milton's
character certainly sets a precedent for Melville's master of disguises used for evil purposes. But these parallels apply mostly to the first part of the book and have
been grossly overemphasized by those who represent
The Confidence-Man as a simple allegory in which the
central character is the Devil. The Shakespearean significances are more ambiguous because, as we have seen,
the confidence man, as a character, does not resemble
Hamlet, whom Melville admired as an "original" literary creation, but Autolycus, in whom he was more simply interested. The quixotic significances, however, are
more revealing. Lunatic or idealist, Don Quixote was to
Melville a symbol of opposition to the materialistic "green
grocer" wisdom that he satirized in the confidence man
himself in the first half of the book and in the characters
with whom the confidence man plays his discursive
quixotic game in the last half. Melville's attitude toward his work was more like that of Cervantes than it
was like either of the other authors, Milton and Shakespeare, whom he tried to emulate; and it was this attitude that gave his book its most pervasive unity.

For there was not only a "Drummond light" but also a
"hidden sun" in *The Confidence-Man*, such as the
cosmopolitan found in Shakespeare's plays. This was, as
in the plays, the author himself. Although the book was
dominated by a central character, the consistency of its
view of the world is to be found in those concerns with

what Melville called his "comedy of thought" as well as his "comedy of action" (71).

Melville's intrusion of himself into his book is most evident in those three chapters in which he stands aside from his story and attempts to explain, justify, or apologize for his central character. But it is more subtly revealed in other sections over which the confidence man exercises little or no control—especially in the interpolated short stories and in some of the discursive passages in which Melville seems to be speaking through his characters rather than allowing them to speak entirely for themselves. The stories most clearly reveal how Melville subtly wove his own emotional and intellectual concerns into the texture of his otherwise detached narrative and show why he admired both Don Quixote and Hamlet as truly "original" characters. Both were mad in the eyes of the world, as Melville himself was sometimes thought to be, but for Don Quixote as well as for Hamlet (as Melville suggested in his poem "The Rusty Man") the time was out of joint, and the antic disposition he himself put on in writing his most important but least popular novels was, as he had suggested in a letter on 1 June 1851 to Hawthorne, a reaction to circumstances rather than to the Gospels. The consistent satire in *The Confidence-Man* was directed against the worldliness of the times, not against trust, however absurdly it might be, under some circumstances, misplaced.

Moreover, *The Confidence-Man* is an ambitious book. The subtle and various means by which Melville achieved a high level of ironic ambiguity, the crispness of his style (which even those who discredit the book as a whole have found admirable),[4] and his attempts to create a genuinely original character in the cosmopolitan all testify to Melville's high literary ambitions. Yet Melville's achievements exist mostly beneath the surface of his narrative, and it is the surface of this novel that has disturbed many readers who brought to it conventional expectations and found them disappointed.

Newton Arvin complained that "narratively speaking, *The Confidence-Man* is meager and monotonous" because it does not "move."[5] Similarly, F. O. Matthiessen objected to the "incessant hammering" of Melville's thoughts and concluded that structurally *The Confidence-Man* is "no more than a manipulated pattern of abstractions."[6] And Roy Fuller, John Shroeder, and Warner Berthoff have all remarked on the "single-mindedness" with which the author dealt with his material—though they do not agree on the object of Melville's obsessiveness.[7]

These criticisms of the book are perhaps valid if it is treated strictly as a conventional narrative. It does not "move"; as R. W. B. Lewis has observed, "at first glance, it seems rather to bulge and thicken than to progress."[8] And it does appear to be a disturbingly "single-minded" production. But this book, unlike most of Melville's earlier works, does not place its emphasis upon movement—in particular, upon a voyage—though Melville's earliest intention for it, as indicated by the discarded fragment "The River," may have been been in that direction. Nor do the actions of its hero revolve around the obsessive pursuit of an object, either of love, hate, or justice, as the actions of the heroes of *Mardi, Moby-Dick,* and *Pierre* did. Melville had rejected his customary method of spinning a "yarn" in favor of developing the "significances" suggested by the provocative actual swindler who had prompted the invention of the term *confidence man.* Though the narrative of this book may be thin and insubstantial, that does not necessarily suggest that Melville's talents had reached an "ebb."[9] *The Confidence-Man* churns internally; it is a mulling over, a series of variations upon a theme. And whatever energy and imagination are active in it do not primarily present themselves either in the unraveling of events or in a direct commentary on or an interpretation of those events.

Approached as novel, romance, allegory, or even simple satire, *The Confidence-Man* reveals a great many
defects. One is apt to conclude with a contemporary
reviewer—who claimed to have read parts of the book
forward and parts backward, to have attacked it then in
the middle, and finally to have read it beginning to end—
that, all in all, *The Confidence-Man* is a "sad jumble."[10]
It is a mistake, however, to approach this book exclu-
sively in terms of its narrative; for, as Warner Berthoff
has suggested, "the deepest meaning of the book is the
atmosphere of mind it registers and proceeds from. Deeper
than the satirical 'comedy of thought' that, for one thing,
never tells us, as such comedies customarily do, what
grounds of fictive abstractions the events and characters
are meant to occupy."[11]

In form, then, *The Confidence-Man* might more ac-
curately be described as what Northrop Frye has called
the "Menippean satire," or "anatomy." The anatomy, as
Frye explains, "deals less with people as such than with
mental attitudes. Pedants, bigots, cranks, parvenus, vir-
tuosi, enthusiasts, rapacious and incompetent professional
men of all kinds are handled in terms of their occupa-
tional approach to life as distinct from their social behavior."[12] It differs from the romance in that

> it is not primarily concerned with the exploits of heroes,
> but relies on the free play of intellectual fancy and the kind
> of humorous observation that produces caricature. It dif-
> fers also from the picaresque form, which has the novel's
> interest in the actual structure of society. At its most
> concentrated the Menippean satire presents us with a vision
> of the world in terms of a single intellectual pattern. The
> intellectual structure built up from the story makes for
> violent dislocations in the customary logic of narrative,
> though the appearance of carelessness that results reflects
> only the carelessness of the reader or his tendency to judge
> by a novel-centered conception of fiction.[13]

Melville may have been drawn toward this mode of fiction inadvertently through his continued speculation
on his central character, who supplied his book with a

unifying device for its episodic narrative, and his preoccupation with a "single intellectual pattern"—the problem of confidence. But Burton's *Anatomy of Melancholy* (which provided Frye with his term for Menippean satire) had been an important influence on *Mardi* and was in Melville's mind soon after his completion of *The Confidence-Man*. He visited his friend Evert Duyckinck in October 1856 and, during an evening's lively conversation filled with the "jargon of things unknowable," "instanced old Burton as atheistical—in the exquisite irony of his passages on some sacred matters."[14] Whether or not Melville found in Burton's anatomy a precedent for his own, he could appreciate its exquisite irony, for he had just been practicing a similar sort of irony in his own book.

Though for the most part contemporary reviewers viewed *The Confidence-Man* as a novel and found fault with its narrative, at least one reviewer approved it because it was not a novel. The reviewer for the *New-York Evening Times* identified Melville's book not as a novel but as a "Rabelaisian patchwork":

> Mr. Melville's *Confidence-Man* is almost as ambiguous an apparition as his *Pierre*, who was altogether an impossible and ununderstandable creature. But, in the *Confidence-Man*, there is no attempt at a novel, or a romance, for Melville has not the slightest qualifications for a novelist, and therefore he appears to much better advantage here than in his attempts at story books. . . . It is, in short, a Rabelaisian piece of patchwork without any of the Rabelaisian indecency. . . . The oddities of thought, felicities of expression, and wit, humor, and rollicking inspirations are as abundant and original as in any of the productions of this most remarkable writer.[15]

Rabelais's story of *Gargantua and Pantagruel* is, of course, another work that Frye cites as an example of this type of fiction, and it is significant that one early reviewer as well as such a sensitive modern critic as Berthoff identified *The Confidence-Man* as being in the uncommon but not unprecedented category to which it belongs.

The deepest meaning of the book must therefore be sought in the attitude of mind it "registers and proceeds from"—or rather, in view of the fact that the book grew and changed as it was written, the attitude of mind that proceeded from the significances Melville found in his material.

At some undetermined time, Melville scored a passage in his Bible that clarifies to some extent his ambivalent attitude toward religious faith and hints at the "vital truth" he had detected in Lear and now dramatized in this novel: "Let no man deceive himself. If any man among you seemeth to be wise in this world, let him become a fool, that he may be wise" (I Corinthians 3:18).[16] These verses immediately follow: "For the wisdom of this world is foolishness with God: for it is written, He taketh the wise in their own craftiness. And again, The Lord knoweth the thoughts of the wise, that they are vain" (I Corinthians 3:19–20). All three are significant because the paradoxical relation between the wisdom of the world and heavenly wisdom had apparently troubled Melville for some time. In *Moby-Dick* he had written that "man's insanity is heaven's sense," and in *Pierre* he had paraphrased the Pauline passage and provided its converse formulation: "And thus, though the earthly wisdom of man be heavenly folly to God; so also, conversely, is the heavenly wisdom of God an earthly folly to man."[17] The same sort of ambiguity that characterized the Plinlimmon pamphlet in *Pierre* is evident in *The Confidence-Man.*

It is this sort of ambiguity, dramatized and illustrated rather than discussed, that makes *The Confidence-Man* so puzzling. If faith was the heavenly wisdom of God and could be an earthly folly to man, it could be easily victimized by anyone wise in his own craftiness—as the confidence man was in his masquerade throughout the first half of the book. The many characters he tricked and duped were certainly lacking in worldly wisdom and are not held up for admiration.[18] On the contrary, they may be the pitiable "victims of auto da fe" to whom the book was in part, if not as a whole, "dedicated."[19] Yet when the same man who seemed to be so wise in this world in the first part of the book became a fool (dressed in at least a suggestion of motley) in the second, he showed up the pretentious "wisdom" of the transcendentalists and the false geniality of the "boon companion" as being thoroughly contemptible.

Hawthorne probably came closest to defining Melville's position in the midst of this ambiguity when he reported on their long walk on the outskirts of Liverpool after the book was finished but before it was published. "He had 'pretty much made up his mind to be annihilated,'" Hawthorne reported, "but still he does not seem to rest in that anticipation."[20] "He could neither believe, nor be comfortable in his unbelief"; he had persisted as long as Melville's friend had known him in wandering over intellectual deserts that Hawthorne considered as dismal as the sand hills amid which they were sitting.

Melville may also have been suggesting his own situation in another identification of himself with Don Quixote. One of the passages he marked in Cervantes's book reads, "a knight errant without a mistress is like a tree without leaves, a building without cement, a shadow without a body that causes it." Melville's comment was, "X or as Confucius said 'a dog without a master,' or to drop both Cervantes & Confucius parables—a god-like mind without a God."[21] In any event, he was sure in his own mind that the thoughts of the worldly wise were vain.

A more positive expression of the state of mind to which he clung so long may be found in his "Epilogue" to *Clarel*, published twenty years after his conversation with Hawthorne. The poem was another "anatomy of faith" written after Melville's own persistent intellectual and emotional wanderings had been publicly symbolized in the conflict of science and religion. "Ape and Angel" had become new symbols in the "strife and old debate," but Melville had not yet renounced his need for faith; in the religious terminology he had evidently used in his conversations with Hawthorne, he was able to advise his distressed young student of theology:

> Then keep thy heart, though yet but ill resigned.
> Clarel, thy heart, the issues there but mind;
> That like a crocus budding through the snow—
> That like a swimmer rising from the deep—
> That like a burning secret which doth go
> Even from the bosom that would hoard and keep
> Emerge thou mayst from the last whelming sea,
> And prove that death but routs life into victory.[22]

This is guessing; and however useful such guessing may be in casting light upon the obscurity of Melville's inner vision, the last chapters of *The Confidence-Man* illuminate the "atmosphere" of Melville's mind and testify to his range of thought and feeling. In shorter compass, we may observe in these chapters the same sort of unevenness of mood (alternately playful and morose, delighted and despairing) as in the two most telling accounts of Melville's state of mind after he had completed *The Confidence-Man*. Evert Duyckinck characterized Melville's visit to his home in October 1856 as a "good stirring evening—ploughing deep and bringing to the surface rich fruits of thoughts and experience"; but Hawthorne recorded Melville's visit with him the next month as a display of his "morbid state of mind," though Melville himself remembered of their afternoon walk and conversation "a strong wind" and "good talk" and, in the evening, "Stout and Fox and Geese."[23] Hawthorne no doubt identified his dominant mood, but Melville was capable, it appears, of intellectual excitement, deeply felt sympathy, and normal good fun as well, if only intermittently. The comic Melville is to be found in the barber episode in chapters 42 and 43, and the quality of his sympathy in the "increase in seriousness" of the final chapter. These last chapters brighten, even if they do not eliminate, the dark picture that most critics have painted of Melville at this period of his career.

Alert as modern readers are to the "blackness" in *The Confidence-Man*, they are perhaps apt to miss the lighter features of this "comedy of thought and action." His nineteenth-century readers, on the other hand, though they might miss his deeper meanings, probably caught the humor of chapters 42 and 43, where the cosmopolitan encounters the boat's barber. This episode, like every other in the second half of the book with the single exception of the brief encounter with Pitch in chapter 24, dramatizes the meeting of one confidence man with another, though, as we have seen, the transcendentalists were confidence men only by satiric implication.

The probable source of inspiration for this episode is to be found in the same issue of *Harper's* that printed Melville's story "Jimmy Rose" in November 1855 and that the author no doubt had on hand. It was described in the table of contents as a "Barberised Drama," and the editor prefaced the sketch with the observation that among the "greatest bores" in any large city is "your *keen barber*, who with '*speculation* in his eyes'; the moment you enter his shop to enjoy a hasty shave, prepares to make a 'customer' of you in more shapes than one. It is very rarely that these tonsorial Jeremy Diddlers get '*come over*' more triumphantly than was the subject of the following sketch—in itself a double satire, in manner and in theme."[24]

The brief one-act play that follows his remarks is a playful sketch in which Oily, the barber, unsuccessfully tries to diddle his customer, Jones. Jones is immune to the blandishments of the barber (his "oil") and drily resists the barber's attempts to sell him his "Vegetable Extract," a wig, and various brushes, soaps, and scents. The haircut completed, Jones, to the frustrated befuddlement of Oily, pays and asks to be shown the door. The drama concludes with the barber saying to his man:

> That's a rare customer, at any rate.
> Had I cut him as short as he cut me,
> How little hair upon his head would be!

The most compelling parallel between this dramatic sketch and the cosmopolitan's encounter with the barber on the *Fidèle* is the similarity of their conclusions. Oily identifies Jones as a "rare customer," and William Cream remembers Goodman as a "queer customer," though Cream's friends after they are told about him dub the cosmopolitan "quite an original." And this last phrase provided the occasion for the narrator to interrupt his narrative with his remarks about original characters in chapter 44. But there are other parallels as well. Melville, perhaps deriving the name for his barber from the name *Oily*, named his own creation *Cream*. There exists in Melville's treatment, though more thoroughly and creatively, the same sort of punning as is found in both the drama and, more particularly, in the editor's preface. The *Harper's* editor called attention to his own punning with cant terms by means of italics and quotation marks: Oily is both *"keen"* in the sense of being shrewd and something of a sharper; he has *"speculation* in his eyes," and a *speculator* was, in nineteenth-century cant, a general term for any sort of rogue; Oily is *come over* by Jones—that is, Jones cheats or overreaches the barber; the barber plans to make a *customer* of Jones, and this term identified any thief's victim; and this "barberised" drama has a punning reference both to the slang verb *to barber*, or for one thief to cheat another, and the noun, which denotes any sort of thief, as well as gossipy conversation generally.[25] Finally and most importantly, the humor of Melville's episode depends upon the recognition that, like Oily, the barber is himself a type of confidence man with designs upon the cosmopolitan.

The barber episode is not another "devil's joke," as some would have it, but pure comedy, a battle of wits in which the cosmopolitan earns the title "man-charmer—as certain East Indians are called snake-charmers," and William Cream is the snake.[26] It is a highly dramatized encounter introduced in part by Egbert's recollection in the previous chapter that "All the world's a stage / And

all the men and women merely players, / Who have their
exits and their entrances." Frank Goodman's apparent
frustration with the hardened Egbert caused him to drop
his "fictitious character" and speak his true disgust at
the transcendentalist's lack of charity, but he picks that
character up again with his entrance into the barber's
shop. From the very beginning, their dialogue is a tissue
of misunderstandings and double meaning, the wit of
which largely derives from a punning with underworld
jargon.

The cosmopolitan asks the barber if he is competent
to give him a "good shave"—that is, the reader is meant
to understand, is he capable of cheating him? (*Shaver*
meant a "cunning cheat, a subtle fellow"). The barber
responds with the curious remark, "No broker more so,
sir." The cosmopolitan appears ignorant of the term *broker* as an appropriate application to the present situation, but Melville assumed that his readers would understand that a *broker* was a pandering retailer akin to a
Yankee peddler. "Broker?" queries the cosmopolitan, "What
has a broker to do with lather? A broker I have always
understood to be a worthy dealer in certain papers and
metals" (226). The barber finds this question humorous,
for if he does not know what brokers have to do with
lather, he certainly knows what barbers have to do with
papers and metals.

From that point forward, the episode is a witty exchange of double and triple entendre, the full meaning
of which neither interlocutor seems to fully comprehend but which was intended to delight the reader. The
cosmopolitan argues the virtues of confidence and im-
portunes the barber to remove his sign of No Trust. The
barber, on the other hand, firmly resists his pleading but
gradually begins to recognize that his *customer* might
be doubly *shaved* by going security for this gesture of
confidence in man. When he learns that the cosmopolitan is a "philanthropist" (230), the barber becomes "almost as sociable as if the heating water were meant for
whiskey-punch" instead of shaving lather (231). The as-

sociation between the water and whiskey recalls the previous encounter with Charlie Noble where wine had the same function—to muddle the brain of the cosmopolitan and thus make an easy victim of him. In this case, however, the punch is meant, literally and figuratively, for the *lather* necessary to complete the *shave.*

It is the *lather,* or smooth talk, on both sides that constitutes the comedy of this episode, as Melville reminds us through repeated puns. When the cosmopolitan notices the No Trust sign and bursts out with "By my heart, sir! but at least you are valiant, backing the spleen of Thersites with the pluck of Agamemnon," the barber, "hopeless of his customer" because he cannot understand him, replies, "Your sort of talk, sir, is not exactly in my line" (226). The phrase *in my line* is repeated three times, almost in succession, and it refers at once to the bachelor's incapacity to catch Goodman's meaning and to the *line* a swindler uses to dupe a victim.

This sort of intellectual wordplay continues throughout. The barber attempts to *brush up* his *customer*— that is, to flatter him—and to apply his own *lather.* But he also recognizes the cosmopolitan's talent for smooth talk and, in an effort to put an end to Goodman's pleas to remove the sign, applies the shaving cream: "'Ah, sir, all people ain't like you,' was the smooth reply, at the same time, as if smoothly to close the debate, beginning smoothly to apply the lather, which operation, however, was, by a motion, protested against by the subject." The cosmopolitan continues to preach against the barber's lack of trust, thus preventing the barber from shaving him. In yet another witty pun, the barber once more attempts to silence his customer: "Very true, sir, and upon my honor, sir, you talk very well. But the lather is getting cold, sir" (227).

The cosmopolitan's excessive address of William Cream as *barber,* though appropriate to his occupation, is also meant to characterize him as a thief (the slang meaning of *barber*) who would shave him in more ways than one.

And Cream is meant to be a worthy adversary for the eloquent Frank Goodman; he is described as "shrewd," "sly," and "cunning" (234), and he holds that the barber's trade has taught him that all men are deceptive, in appearance and in heart. Moreover, the barber stands to gain fifty dollars (or so he believes) from the cosmopolitan by having him go security for an experiment in trust. Cream, in fact, reminds Goodman of that when the cosmopolitan attempts to restore the barber's confidence in man:

> "You mean, sir, you would have me try the experiment of taking down that notification," again pointing to it with his brush; "but, dear me, while I sit chatting here, the water boils over."
> With which words, and such a well-pleased, sly, snug expression, *as they say some men have when they think their little stratagem has succeeded,* he hurried to the copper vessel, and soon had his cup foaming up with bubbles, as if it were a mug of new ale. (233–34; italics supplied)

It is Cream, not Goodman, who reintroduces the topic of removing his sign of No Trust, though he had feigned disinterest before. The "magical" qualities of persuasion the narrator assigns to Goodman after the completion of the shave are practiced on a more than willing victim, despite the "earnest protest" he apparently pretends.

William Cream agrees to remove his sign of No Trust but insists that they have an agreement in writing insuring that the cosmopolitan will cover any losses the barber might suffer by trusting mankind. After the agreement is drafted and signed, Cream makes his play for his security money: " 'Very good,' said the barber, 'and now nothing remains but for me to receive the cash' " (236). Unlike Charlie Noble's reaction to a similar request, which this scene is partly meant to recall, the cosmopolitan displays no surprise at the barber's demands, not only contending that such a request violates the spirit of the contract and therefore refusing the barber the security for the present, but also holding him to the letter of their agreement and refusing to pay for his own shave.

In the end, the cosmopolitan has accomplished his design. He has persuaded the barber to remove his sign, if only momentarily, for Cream replaces it the moment Goodman leaves. And it is fitting that the confidence man should have taken on the barber in this battle of wits and prevailed, for the barber's sign of No Trust, juxtaposed as it had been to the mute's scribbled pleas for charity in the opening chapter, had announced Melville's theme for his book.

Melville's "comedy" is concluded with this episode, and he ambiguously leaves it an even question whether the cosmopolitan is a quixotic simpleton or a knowing cheat. The barber tears up their agreement, "which he felt the more free to do from the impression that in all human probability he would never again see the person who had drawn it" (237). But Melville does not allow his readers to share the barber's certainty: "Whether that impression proved well-founded or not, does not appear" (237). At any rate, in the following chapter Melville speculates on original characters and provides hints about what he had been trying to do in his own book. The final chapter, however, marks an "increase in seriousness." Chapters 42 and 43 were clearly meant to amuse and show Melville to have been capable of comedy without disguised malicious or sacrilegious intent. A diddler is diddled, a shaver shaved, in an ingenious, sometimes brilliant exchange of wit and debate, a comic interlude rivaling like moments of comedy in Shakespeare. But the author's concluding note is a somber one.

In this final chapter the cosmopolitan enters the cabin where the boat's Bible is kept. In that cabin an old man sits reading the "True Book" beneath a solar lamp "whose shade of ground glass was all round fancifully variegated, in transparency, with the image of a horned altar, from which flames rose, alternate with the figure of a robed man, his head encircled by a halo" (240). This

lamp, as Elizabeth Foster has suggested, probably sym-
bolizes the light of scriptural revelation and religious
faith.[27] The light itself "with ever-diminishing distinct-
ness" pervades the cabin, where all but the old man are
abed. All other lamps have been put out, but the remaining one is lit by command of the captain "till the natural
light of day should come to relieve it" (240).

The cosmopolitan, seeking to verify the barber's assertion that certain scriptural passages preach distrust
of man, learns that these passages as well as others to
the same effect are indeed in the Bible. He is distressed
by this until the old man relieves his mind by explaining
that these passages are from the Apocrypha and therefore of "uncertain credit." The two men subsequently
enter into a conversation upon divine "wisdom" and
the notion that "to distrust the creature, is a kind of
distrusting of the Creator" (244). But, for those sleepers
in the dark corners of the cabin, this discussion and the
light itself are nuisances. The lamp is "inwardly blessed
by those in some berths, and inwardly execrated by those
in others" (241), and the discussion of heavenly wisdom
is punctuated with cynical remarks from the darkness.

The cosmopolitan questions the apocryphal Wisdom
of the Son of Sirach and muses that if wisdom advises
man to beware of his fellows, then "What an ugly thing
wisdom must be!" Certain passengers have little use for
such speculation. One complains, "If you two don't know
enough to sleep, don't be keeping wiser men awake. And
if you want to know what wisdom is, go find it under
your blankets." Another shares the sentiment: "To bed
with ye, ye divils, and don't be after burning your fingers
with the likes of wisdom." The old man suggests that he
and the cosmopolitan speak more softly for fear of an-
noying the others. The cosmopolitan gives the suggestion a new twist by replying, "I should be sorry if wisdom annoyed any one" (243–44).

There is a significant implication in Melville's juxtaposition of the earnest inquiry of the old man and the
cosmopolitan with the faceless complaints of passen-

gers who take less interest in "wisdom" than in a good night's sleep. The world at large might well consider such discourse folly, even madness; but the complacent world, like the passengers in their berths, prefers "to sleep, not see" (240). It is this very complacency that is ironically contrasted with the idealistic pair who ponder Scripture, and Melville deepens the irony further by demonstrating how easily the old man, who for seventy-five years had retained his innocence and faith, falls into worldly suspicions.

This occurs when a boy peddler enters the cabin selling various devices that would protect the good Simeon-figure from thieves in the night. This small, sinister drummer, with eyes like "sparks in fresh coal" (244), "leopard-like teeth" (244), and a foot like a "horny hoof" (247), finds the old man an easy mark. The man purchases a door lock and money belt from the boy, and the peddler throws in a counterfeit detector as a bonus. These items, along with the life-preserver that the old man takes to his room, presumably will guarantee him a good night's sleep; he too, it seems, would rather sleep than see.

So far had Melville come to identify with the cosmopolitan in this episode and to prefer a foolish confidence to fearful suspicion that he seems to have felt the need to introduce another sort of rogue in this final chapter. The boy peddler is the complementary opposite of a confidence man, although the knowing wink the boy throws the cosmopolitan but which Goodman does not perceive indicates that the boy believes they are of the same breed. This type of peddler does not prey upon his customer's confidence but upon his fear and distrust of mankind. Like the "lightning-rod man" (whom Melville had represented in a story by the same name, published in *Putnam's*, August 1854), this peddler "travels in storm-time, and drives a brave trade with the fears of man."[28] But his business thrives because successful swindlers who have preyed upon confidence have made even the most innocent and confiding capable of "No Trust."

It is the quality of pity, in Melville, that makes this

chapter rise above satire. For the old man makes a truly pathetic figure as he searches in vain for marks that would indicate the validity of his bank notes and feebly feels his way out of the darkening cabin with his money belt in one hand and the stool life preserver under his arm. He is unaware of the ironic significance of his purchases, however; for, after making them, he agrees with the cosmopolitan that the traveling public ought to trust in the wisdom of the Bible: ". . . for, in all our wanderings through this vale, how pleasant, not less than obligatory, to feel that we need start at no wild alarms, provide for no wild perils; trusting in that Power which is alike able and willing to protect us when we cannot ourselves" (250).The cosmopolitan approves of this sentiment and adds, "The traveler who has not this trust, what miserable misgivings must be his; or, what vain, short-sighted care must he take of himself" (250). It is, of course, vanity and shortsighted care that prompt the old traveler, despite his convictions, to buy the peddler's contraptions and search for a life preserver, which the cosmopolitan locates in the very stool the old man was sitting on and sardonically recommends: "'I think I can recommend this one; the tin part,' rapping it with his knuckles, 'seems so perfect—sounds so very hollow'" (251). Supplied with this final hollow assurance, the old man is kindly led out of the cabin; the waning light of the solar lamp of faith expires, leaving the cabin in total darkness.

The implication of this concluding chapter is that even the most innocent and long-lived faith, as exemplified in the old man, is subject to frailty and the corrosion of fear and suspicion. The light of this faith went out, and although Melville concluded with a suggestion that "Something further may follow of this masquerade," the book as it stands leaves the reader as well as the characters in darkness. The conclusion of this ambiguous book, however, is not altogether dark and bitter. The object of its consistent scorn is neither confidence men nor gullible humanity nor religious faith, but complacency. Melville may have begun it in a mood of cynicism, but he could not long repose comfortably in that mood. The change his satire took in the second half suggests that ultimately he sided with the fool of virtue against the serene and self-satisfied greengrocer, and the final chapter shows that the frailty of innocent virtue should be recorded with charity. The old man is pitiable, not contemptible; and when the cosmopolitan "kindly" leads him out of the cabin, Melville seems once more to be identifying with his title character.

The shift of Melville's mood from the scorn and contempt of the first half of his book to the quality of pity that characterizes this final chapter is essentially a movement from Timonism toward a humane and feeling skepticism. It is a movement toward what Miguel de Unamuno described as the tragic sense of life; and coincidentally Unamuno, perhaps, came closest to articulating the difference between Melville's state of mind when he began his book and when he completed it:

> There are people who seem not to be content with not believing that there is another life, or rather, with believing that there is none, but who are vexed and hurt that others should believe in it or even should wish that it might exist. And this attitude is as contemptible as that is worthy of respect which characterizes those who, though urged by the need they have of it to believe in another life, are unable to believe.[29]

This latter attitude of mind, which is itself incapable of belief but does not begrudge others their faith, reminiscent as it is of Hawthorne's assessment of Melville's dilemma, is, according to Unamuno, the "most noble attitude of the spirit, the most profound, the most human, and the most fruitful, the attitude of despair." Viewed in this light the quality of mind that Melville confessed to after the completion of *The Confidence-Man*, his despair, ought not be taken as a token of his spleen but as an achievement of his heart. Plagued as he was by public neglect, ill health, and financial worry, he could not, or would not forfeit his sympathy for the human condition.

To suggest that the final chapters of *The Confidence-Man* brighten this dark and often bitter book is not to minimize the depth of his religious skepticism or the authenticity of his personal resentment, even as Melville himself surely minimized certain apparently similar doubts and feelings he had had six years before but had described in a letter to Hawthorne as "certain crotchetty and over doleful chimearas." "Men like you and me and some others," he wrote to Hawthorne, "forming a chain of God's posts round the world, must be content to encounter [such feelings] now and then, and fight them the best way we can. But come they will,—for, in the boundless, trackless, but still glorious wild wilderness through which these outposts run, the Indians do sorely abound, as well as the insignificant but still stinging mosquitoes."[30] Certainly, by the time he came to write *The Confidence-Man*, his doubts were more savage and the wilderness less glorious; but a few weeks before he described these "chimearas" he had announced to Hawthorne in another letter, "I stand for the heart. To dogs with the head! I had rather be a fool with a heart, than Jupiter Olympus with his head."[31] This quality, too, had persisted in Melville, as much as his unbelief had persisted. And though at times his sympathies might have been in eclipse, they were as obdurate as his doubts.

In the end, *The Confidence-Man* offers no easy affirmations, but neither is it a mean-spirited, fragmented, chaotic book. Rather, it is a clear-eyed consideration of the ambiguous problem of faith as it relates to the daily lives of men, the men of "flesh and bone" as Unamuno would have it. Faith was often impracticable, but without it man was cold and contemptible. It was frail at best, and all too often a light that failed. But however sardonic Melville may have been about Christian "gifts" and however uncertain he may have been of hope, in the end he achieved and attributed to his confidence man the greatest of all Christian virtues—that of charity. And in so doing, he brought his rambling narrative around into a complete circle. Although ultimately he may have failed to achieve the high literary ambitions he had for it, Melville's anatomy of faith is ample proof that the author had not lost his talents as a writer, nor, in the end, his heart as a man.

Notes

Introduction

1. Reprinted in Chester L. Davis, "Mark Twain's Religious Beliefs as Indicated by Notations in His Books," p. 3.
2. Poem "1551," in *The Complete Poems of Emily Dickinson*, ed. Thomas H. Johnson, p. 646.
3. Richard Chase, "An Approach to Melville" and "Melville's Confidence Man."
4. Hershel Parker, Foreword to the Norton Critical Edition of *The Confidence-Man*, p. ix.
5. Herman Melville, *The Confidence-Man: His Masquerade* (Evanston & Chicago: Northwestern University Press and the Newberry Library, 1982), p. 68. Parenthetical citations in the text are to this edition.

Chapter 1: Significances

1. This, the Clifford enclosure, and two succeeding letters on the same subjects are printed in full in Herman Melville, *The Letters of Herman Melville*, eds. Merrell R. Davis and William H. Gilman, pp. 153–63. Hereafter cited as *Letters*.
2. For a discussion of this, see Harrison Hayford, "The Significance of Melville's 'Agatha' Letters."
3. *Letters*, p. 140.
4. See Leon Howard, *Herman Melville: A Biography*, p. 197.
5. *Letters*, p. 157.
6. Ibid., pp. 155–57.
7. Ibid., p. 156.
8. Ibid., p. 157.
9. Ibid., p. 157.
10. Ibid., p. 157; italics added.
11. Ibid., p. 157.
12. Herman Melville, *Redburn: His First Voyage*, p. 125.
13. See chap. 91, "The Pequod Meets the Rose-Bud," *Moby-Dick*, pp. 336–42.
14. See Jay Leyda, *The Melville Log: A Documentary Life of Herman Melville*, 2:507.
15. Herman Melville, *Great Short Works of Herman Melville*, ed. Warner Berthoff, p. 354.
16. Melville, *Letters*, p. 170.
17. See Howard, *Herman Melville*, p. 209.
18. Leyda, *Log*, 2:500–501.

19. Ibid., 2:506. Those novels were *Waikna; or Adventures on the Mosquito Shore* by Samuel A. Bard (pseud. for George Ephraim Squier; see Merton Sealts's *Melville's Reading: A Checklist of Books Owned and Borrowed*, entry 485) and *Panama in 1855* by Robert Tomes (Sealts, entry 528).

20. Ibid., 2:508.

21. Ibid.

22. Howard, *Herman Melville*, pp. 227–28.

23. A transcription of "The River" is printed in the Norton Critical Edition of *The Confidence-Man*, ed. Hershel Parker, pp. 222–23.

24. Melville's manuscript "Titles for Chapters" are printed in an appendix to Elizabeth Foster's edition of *The Confidence-Man* (New York: Hendricks House, 1954), pp. 380–84.

25. Elsewhere ("Two Sources in *The Confidence-Man*," *Melville Society Extracts* 39 [September 1979]: 12–13), I have suggested that Melville's "hearing" of an author who might produce a "score" of originals in a single work has probable reference to a review of Dickens's *Bleak House* in the November 1853 issue of *Putnam's*. In that review, the anonymous reviewer argued that the creation of "new" characters in fiction was extremely rare but that Dickens created such characters by the dozens. Melville's attention might have been drawn to this issue of *Putnam's* when he was reading proof for *The Piazza Tales* from his copies of *Putnam's* early in 1856; the review immediately followed the conclusion of the first part of "Bartleby the Scrivener" as it appeared in the magazine.

26. Warner Berthoff, *The Example of Melville*, p. 60.

Chapter 2: The Man in Town

1. This newspaper article is reprinted in Johannes Bergmann's "The Original Confidence-Man: The Development of the American Confidence Man in the Sources and Backgrounds of Herman Melville's *The Confidence-Man: His Masquerade*," p. 227. As will be noted, most of the factual material in this chapter has been derived from Bergmann's fine dissertation.

2. Reprinted in Bergmann, "The Original Confidence-Man," p. 204.

3. The editor of the *Knickerbocker* applauded the *Herald* satire and informed his readers that he would have reprinted the article entire except for "the fact that it has been widely circulated" (quoted in Bergmann, "The Original Confidence-Man," p. 213). It is interesting to note that the author might assume a general familiarity with the piece and the currency of the subject matter two months after the original publication of the item in the *Herald*.

4. Paul Smith first located this article and reprinted it in his "*The Confidence-Man* and the Literary World of New York." The article is

also reprinted in Bergmann, "The Original Confidence-Man," pp. 213–14, and in the Norton edition of *The Confidence-Man*, pp. 227–28.

5. The *New York Herald*, the *Spirit of the Times*, and the *Albion* gave the drama approving reviews and testified to the play's success. See Bergmann, "The Original Confidence-Man," pp. 217–18.

6. There is no evidence that Melville attended this interlude. However, *The Confidence Man* was widely reviewed, and Melville could have easily read or heard of the play's success. If he was familiar with the play, his own literary use of the confidence man six years later may have been calculated to cash in on a subject that had already proved popular with the American public. Far from being Melville's "valedictory," as Charles Feidelson has suggested in his *Symbolism and American Literature*, p. 208, *The Confidence-Man*, at least in subject matter, seems to have been designed to win public approval.

7. See Leon Howard, *Herman Melville: A Biography*, p. 150.

8. Quoted in Bergmann, "The Original Confidence-Man," pp. 221–22.

9. Ibid., p. 223.

10. Jay Leyda's *The Melville Log: A Documentary Life of Herman Melville* quotes many reviewers who felt that Melville was squandering his talents. For example, a reviewer of *Moby-Dick* in July 1853 implored Melville to live up to his promise: "O author of 'Typee' and 'Omoo,' we admire so cordially the proven capacity of your pen, that we entreat you to doff the 'non-natural sense' of your late lucubrations—to put off your worser self—and to do your better, real self, that justice which its 'potentiality' deserves" (*Log*, 1:477–78); and a review of *Pierre* in July 1852 comments: "We say it with grief—it is too bad for Mr. Melville to abuse his really fine talents as he does" (*Log*, 1:456).

11. The article is reprinted in the Norton Critical Edition of *The Confidence-Man*, pp. 227–28.

12. In addition to suggesting several English literary characters who may have influenced Melville's creation, including such figures as Chaucer's Pardoner, Shakespeare's Autolycus, Jonson's Mosca and Volpone, and Fielding's Jonathan Wild, Bergmann explores a variety of American scoundrels, both fictional and real, who might have served as influences. His treatment of American confidence men is organized geographically: there are separate chapters on knaves and rogues in New England, the Southwest, and New York City, and there is an entire chapter on the original confidence man, of whom Bergmann has given by far the most extensive and thorough treatment to date.

13. Bergmann, "The Original Confidence-Man," pp. 78–80.

14. Ted N. Weissbuch, in his "A Note on the Confidence-Man's Counterfeit Detector," has demonstrated that counterfeit detectors were widely used in Melville's time—out of necessity.

15. Melville had earlier satirized miraculous inventions of this kind in "The Happy Failure: A Story of the River Hudson," which appeared in *Harper's* in July 1854. In this instance, the object of ridicule is the "Great Hydraulic-Hydrostatic Apparatus," designed for draining swamps.

16. Elizabeth Foster, *The Confidence-Man* (New York: Hendricks House, 1954), p. 318n.

17. Ibid., p. 307n.

18. See Bergmann, "The Original Confidence-Man," pp. 126–29 *passim*.

19. In "The Man That Was Used Up," Poe had portrayed another sham soldier, General Smith, whose fine figure was nothing but a composite of false limbs, a wig, and a glass eye. And James Russell Lowell's character Birdofredum Sawin Esq. claims to have lost an arm, a leg, and an eye in combat.

20. Admittedly, those critics who take the confidence man to be the Devil, such as Elizabeth Foster, Daniel Hoffman, Hershel Parker, and John Shroeder, have good reason to be disturbed, for why would the Devil waste his time trying to gull another swindler or, perhaps, even a fellow devil? John Shroeder, for example, in his "Sources and Symbols for Melville's *Confidence-Man*," confesses that he has no "explanation as to why Noble and Goodman, if both are from the pit, should unknown to one another carry on their long conversation" (p. 315).

21. Watson Branch, "The Genesis, Composition, and Structure of *The Confidence-Man*."

22. According to the *Oxford English Dictionary*, "Charlie" was a mid-nineteenth-century slang term for a "thimble-rigger"—a sleight-of-hand artist who cheated his victims by pretending to hide a pea under a thimble. Melville had used this term earlier in its other underworld sense of "watchman" (see *A Dictionary of the Underworld*) in *Redburn*, p. 196.

23. Harrison Hayford, in his "Poe in *The Confidence-Man*," argues that this figure is a caricature of Edgar Allan Poe.

24. Many critics have argued that Winsome and Egbert are also portraits either of the two sides of Emerson or of Emerson and Thoreau respectively. See, for example, Egbert Oliver's "Melville's Picture of Emerson and Thoreau in *The Confidence-Man*."

25. Quoted in Bergmann, "The Original Confidence-Man," p. 214, and reprinted in the Norton Critical Edition of *The Confidence-Man*, pp. 227–28.

26. Carl Van Vechten, "The Later Work of Herman Melville," p. 283.

Chapter 3: Melville's Antihero

1. Although there is some agreement that the confidence man

masquerades as the mute in cream colors, Black Guinea, the man with the weed, the man in gray, the man in the traveling cap, the herb doctor, the P.I.O. man, and the cosmopolitan, some critics, Elizabeth Foster for example, do not believe that the mute is actually the confidence man ("Introduction," *The Confidence-Man* [New York: Hendricks House, 1954], p. liii); and, more recently, Elizabeth Keysor has argued, in "'Quite an Original': The Cosmopolitan in *The Confidence-Man*," that Frank Goodman does not participate in the masquerade.

2. Philip Drew, "Appearance and Reality in Melville's *The Confidence-Man*."

3. Ibid., p. 422.

4. As Elizabeth Foster points out, "the magazines were full of jokes and cartoons about servants employed through intelligence offices," but she also observes that Melville was familiar with Hawthorne's story "The Intelligence Office" ("Introduction," p. 324n.).

5. Foster, "Introduction," p. lxxi.

6. Jay Leyda, *The Melville Log: A Documentary Life of Herman Melville*, 2:571.

7. See, for example, Foster, "Introduction," p.lxxi, or Watson Branch, "The Genesis, Composition, and Structure of *The Confidence-Man*."

8. Foster, "Introduction," p. lii.

9. See H. Bruce Franklin's *The Wake of the Gods: Melville's Mythology*, p. 159, or Daniel G. Hoffman's *Form and Fable in American Fiction*, pp. 294–95.

10. Ibid., p. 291. Hoffman observes that Melville alluded to Mather's work in "The Lightning-Rod Man" (*Putnam's*, August 1854; Hoffman mistakenly writes that the story appeared in *Harper's*) and "The Apple-Tree Table" (*Putnam's*, May 1856).

11. See Paschal Reeves's "The 'Deaf Mute' Confidence Man: Melville's Impostor in Action."

12. Foster, "Introduction," p. xlviii.

13. See John Shroeder's "Sources and Symbols for Melville's *Confidence-Man*"; Hershel Parker in the foreword and notes to the Norton edition of *The Confidence-Man*; Hoffman's *Form and Fable in American Fiction*, pp. 279–313; Foster's "Introduction"; Leslie Fiedler's "Out of the Whale," p. 494; Lawrance Thompson's *Melville's Quarrel with God*, pp. 297–328; and Malcolm O. Magaw's "*The Confidence-Man* and Christian Deity: Melville's Imagery of Ambiguity."

14. Hershel Parker, Foreword to the Norton Critical Edition of *The Confidence-Man*, p. ix.

15. Shroeder, for instance, has found the Missouri bachelor "theologically sound" because he is the "hardest nut that the confidence man has to crack" ("Sources and Symbols," p. 308).

16. Foster, "Introduction," p. xlix.

17. Shroeder, "Sources and Symbols," pp. 305–6.

18. Hoffman, *Form and Fable*, p. 292.

19. Hershel Parker, "The Metaphysics of Indian-hating," pp. 165–73.

20. For a separate treatment of this aspect of *The Confidence-Man*, see my "Saint Paul's Types of the Faithful and Melville's Confidence Man."

21. Elizabeth Foster points out the relation: "If He hears us, He gives no sign. The Voice of our God is Silence. That is why the lamblike man is deaf and dumb" ("Introduction," p. li).

22. Melville had alluded to this "Pentecostal" conception of speaking in tongues (Acts 2:4) on p. 42. The pantomime in Melville's day, incidentally, was not necessarily a dumb show.

23. See Foster's edition of *The Confidence-Man*, pp. 375–77. Melville had either made or permitted similar changes in the revised version of *Typee*.

24. See Merton Sealts's *Melville's Reading: A Checklist of Books Owned and Borrowed*, entry 62.

25. Ibid., entries 409–10.

26. Leyda, *Log*, 1:276–77.

27. Melville's eyesight prohibited extensive reading or writing by candlelight; as a result, he typically joined in the family entertainments of conversation, cards, or reading aloud in the evenings. See Leon Howard, *Herman Melville: A Biography*, p. 109.

28. Ernest Hemingway, *Death in the Afternoon*, p. 191.

29. Eric Partridge, ed., *A Dictionary of the Underworld*, s.v. "man of the world."

Chapter 4: Literary Models

1. Both Elizabeth Foster and Hershel Parker, in the notes to their respective editions of *The Confidence-Man*, have indicated the frequent instances of serpent imagery as well as other references that they feel link the confidence man to Satan.

2. Henry F. Pommer, *Milton and Melville*, p. 90.

3. The italics in both quotations are Pommer's. Other allusions to Milton that Pommer has identified are given in the notes to the Norton edition of *The Confidence-Man*.

4. Thomas McHaney, in his "*The Confidence-Man* and Satan's Disguises in *Paradise Lost*," identifies additional allusions to Milton's Satan, particularly in the episodes in which the mute appears, and argues that, in his disguise as the mute as well as in all of his other disguises, the confidence man is "always to be identified with the devil." However, as we have noted earlier, Melville's central character is too rich and complex to justify such a simple and pervasive identification, despite the occasional similarities to Satan.

5. Pommer points out the parallels, *Milton and Melville*, p. 64.

6. Quoted in Johannes Bergmann, "The Original Confidence-Man: The Development of the American Confidence Man in the Sources and Backgrounds of Herman Melville's *The Confidence-Man: His Masquerade*," p. 212.

7. Carolyn Lury Karcher, in her *Shadow Over the Promised Land: Slavery, Race, and Violence in Melville's America*, chap. 7, argues that the question of the confidence man's identity is a question of racial identity and that we do not know whether the figure is a white who masquerades as a black or a black who masquerades as a white.

8. Raymond Long, "The Hidden Sun: A Study of the Influence of Shakespeare on the Creative Imagination of Herman Melville," pp. 217–18.

9. Melville had taken a passage from *Cymbeline* as the epigraph for "The Piazza," which was probably written in February 1856.

10. The *Berkshire County Eagle* reported the fancy dress picnic "a startling novelty in this region" and one in which the Melville family had largely participated: Mrs. Melville had masqueraded as "Cyphernia Donothing," Herman's mother had dressed as a market woman, and Malcolm had come as "Jack the Giant Killer" (Jay Leyda, *The Melville Log: A Documentary Life of Herman Melville*, 2:507); Leon Howard, *Herman Melville: A Biography*, p. 226.

11. Ibid., p. 231.

12. Ibid., p. 232.

13. Long, "The Hidden Sun," p. 231.

14. Ibid., p. 237.

15. Ibid., p. 230.

16. Melville had written the following in vol. 7 of his set of Shakespeare apparently sometime in 1849: "Ego non baptizo te in nominee Patris et / Filii et Spiritus Santi—sed in nomine / Diaboli. Madness is undefinable— / It and right reasons extremes of one. / Not the (black art) Goetic but Theurgic magic—seeks converse with the Intelligence, Power, the Angel" (*Letters*, p. 133n.).

17. Herman Melville, *White-Jacket*, p. 51; Harry Levin, "'Don Quixote' and 'Moby-Dick.'"

18. Merton Sealts, *Melville's Reading: A Checklist of Books Owned and Borrowed*, entry 124.

19. Ibid., entry 125.

20. Herman Melville, *Great Short Works of Herman Melville*, ed. Warner Berthoff, p. 389.

21. Leyda, *Log*, 2:532, 548–49.

22. See Levin, "'Don Quixote' and 'Moby-Dick,'" p. 220.

23. Louis Viardot, "Introduction," *Don Quixote de la Mancha*, 1:xvii.

24. Ibid., p. xxxii.

25. Ibid., p. xl.

26. Ibid., p. xli.

27. Viardot describes the legislative attempts to curb this sort of reading (ibid., pp. xlii–xliii).

28. See, respectively, Egbert S. Oliver, "Melville's Goneril and Fanny Kemble"; Hans-Joachim Lang and Benjamin Lease, "Melville's Cosmopolitan: Bayard Taylor in *The Confidence-Man*"; Jane D. Eberwein, "Joel Barlow and *The Confidence-Man*"; Harrison Hayford, "Poe in *The Confidence-Man*"; Egbert S. Oliver, "Melville's Picture of Emerson and Thoreau in 'The Confidence-Man'"; and Helen Trimpi, "Three of Melville's Confidence Men: William Cullen Bryant, Theodore Parker, and Horace Greeley."

29. See Viardot, "Introduction," p. liii.

30. Ibid.

31. Ibid., p. lv.

32. Ibid., p. liii.

33. Herman Melville, *Pierre*, p. 284.

34. Herman Melville, "The Rusty Man," *Collected Poems*, ed. Howard P. Vincent, p. 377. It is quoted in full on p. 112.

35. Nathalia Wright, *Melville's Use of the Bible*, p. 154.

36. The mute in cream colors also recalls Cervantes's mad knight. The deaf mute resembles Quixote in his lack of authority, his guileless nature, his anachronistic demands, his curious aspect, and his irritating persistence. And, like Quixote, the mute is taken for a madman: "To some observers, the singularity, if not lunacy, of the stranger was heightened by his muteness" (5). The perseverance of the man in cream colors in tracing the gospel on his slate naturally irritates certain passengers, since, "perceiving no badge of authority about him," they take him for "some strange kind of simpleton." Moreover, the mute's aspect appears to them as "somehow inappropriate to the time and place" (4), as does his writing. And reminiscent of Don Quixote, the mute is mistreated by those whom he would serve: "They made no scruple to jostle him aside; while one, less kind than the rest, or more of a wag, by an unobserved stroke, dexterously flattened down his fleecy hat upon his head" (4). These Quixote-like qualities of the mute would seem to support the hypothesis that the man in cream colors was a late addition to the confidence man's masquerade. None of the other manifestations of the confidence man, except for the cosmopolitan, bears such a clear resemblance to Cervantes's character. In his other roles, the confidence man is primarily a fraud and a cheat, but in the disguises of the mute and the cosmopolitan the central character displays a quixotic simplicity.

37. See Howard, *Herman Melville*, p. 165.

38. Samuel Taylor Coleridge, *Literary Remains*, 2:207.

Chapter 5: The Personal Element

1. Leon Howard, *Herman Melville: A Biography*, p. 214.

2. *Letters*, p. 170.

3. Melville seems to have taken Montaigne as his authority for the notions that human beings are more often than not "inconsistent," and that authors err when they try to fashion them in a way that passes for consistency. And he seems, as well, to have had Montaigne in mind as that "acutest sage" who is often "at his wits' ends to understand living character" (69). See my "Two Sources in *The Confidence-Man.*"

4. Nathaniel Hawthorne, *The House of the Seven Gables*, 2:1.

5. As I have suggested elsewhere, the germ of this chapter may have been a review of *Bleak House* with which Melville would have become acquainted when he interrupted the composition of *The Confidence-Man* to prepare *The Piazza Tales*. See note 25 for Chapter 1.

6. Hennig Cohen, "Introduction," *The Confidence-Man: His Masquerade* (New York: Holt, Rinehart & Winston, 1964), p. xxiii.

7. Egbert S. Oliver has written about the story of the unfortunate man in his "Melville's Goneril and Fanny Kemble." Paul McCarthy treats the story of the soldier of fortune in "'The Soldier of Fortune' in Melville's *The Confidence-Man.*" The story of the Indian-hater has been discussed by Roy Harvey Pearce, "Melville's Indian Hater: A Note on the Meaning of *The Confidence-Man*"; by Hershel Parker, "The Metaphysics of Indian-hating"; and by William M. Ramsey, "The Moot Points of Melville's Indian-Hating." Carolyn Lury Karcher has written about the story of Charlemont in "The Story of Charlemont: A Dramatization of Melville's Concepts of Fiction in *The Confidence-Man: His Masquerade.*" And Daniel G. Hoffman has discussed "Melville's 'Story of China Aster.'" In addition to these separate treatments, Elizabeth Foster has also discussed each of these stories at some length in her "Introduction" to *The Confidence-Man, passim.*

8. The only previous instance of an interpolated story only tangentially related to the main narrative is Melville's inclusion of "The Town-Ho's Story" in *Moby-Dick*.

9. See Harry Levin's "'Don Quixote' and 'Moby-Dick,'" p. 220.

10. *Adventures of Don Quixote de la Mancha*, 2:277.

11. Howard Vincent has transcribed the subtitle of this poem as "By a Sour One," but Levin believes the manuscript reads "By a Timid One." Levin discusses the varying transcriptions in "'Don Quixote' and 'Moby-Dick,'" p. 226n.

12. Howard, *Herman Melville*, p. 231.

13. See the Norton Critical Edition of *The Confidence-Man*, p. 158n.

14. Howard, *Herman Melville*, p. 231.

15. James Barbour and Robert Sattelmeyer, "A Possible Source and Model for 'The Story of China Aster' in Melville's *The Confidence-Man.*"

16. *Letters*, p. 77.

17. Herman Melville, "Hawthorne and His 'Mosses,'" rpt. in the Norton Critical Edition of *Moby-Dick*, pp. 535–51.

18. The Norton Critical Edition of *The Confidence-Man* provides a wealth of primary material concerning Melville's feelings about Emerson, including relevant letters and the author's annotations of Emerson's *Essays*. See pp. 255–63, *passim*. See also Merton S. Sealts's "Melville and Emerson's Rainbow" for a suggestive examination of Melville's reaction to Emerson.

19. Foster, "Introduction," *The Confidence-Man* (New York: Hendricks House, 1954), pp. lxxiii–lxxxii.

20. Ibid., p. lxxxii.

21. Harrison Hayford, "Poe in *The Confidence-Man*."

22. Ibid., p. 352.

23. A reviewer for *The Southern Quarterly Review*, for instance, had written that Melville's "ravings" in *Moby-Dick* "would justify a write *de lunatico*" (Jay Leyda, *The Melville Log: A Documentary Life of Herman Melville*, 1:496); and a review of *Pierre*, also from the *Southern Quarterly*, suggested that "Herman Melville has gone 'clean daft'" (Leyda, *Log*, 1:463).

Chapter 6: Ignis Fatuus

1. Melville may have taken his cue from Coleridge's "Hamlet" essay in thus fashioning his opening chapter. Coleridge had identified Shakespeare's superior "judgement" in his "management of his first scenes" as an important element of his genius. Such scenes effectively strike the "key-note, and give the predominant spirit of the play" at a glance. See *Literary Remains*, 2:207–8.

2. See Foster's edition of *The Confidence-Man*, p. 377.

3. Newton Arvin, *Herman Melville*, pp. 250–51.

4. F. O. Matthiessen, for example, found the book as a whole "mechanical" but believed that its style is "hard and decisive" (*American Renaissance*, p. 492).

5. Arvin, *Herman Melville*, p. 250.

6. Matthiessen, *American Renaissance*, p. 492.

7. See, respectively, Roy Fuller's "Introduction", *The Confidence-Man* (London: John Lehmann, 1948), pp. v–xiii; John Shroeder's "Sources and Symbols for Melville's *Confidence-Man*"; and Warner Berthoff's "Herman Melville: *The Confidence-Man*."

8. R. W. B. Lewis, "Afterword," *The Confidence-Man* (New York: Signet, 1964), p. 262.

9. In his critical biography *Herman Melville*, Arvin writes that when Melville wrote *The Confidence-Man* "Melville's purely plastic power, his fictive and dramatic power, was at too low an ebb for him to give a rich imaginative embodiment to the things he wished to say" (p. 249).

10. *London Illustrated Times* (25 April 1857); rpt. in the Norton Critical Edition, pp. 275–78.

11. Berthoff, "Herman Melville: *The Confidence-Man,*" p. 234.

12. Northrop Frye, *Anatomy of Criticism: Four Essays,* p. 309. Paul McCarthy, in his "Elements of Anatomy in Melville's Fiction," has also noted that *The Confidence-Man* has a resemblance in form to the anatomy.

13. Frye, *Anatomy of Criticism,* pp. 309–10.

14. Jay Leyda, *The Melville Log: A Documentary Life of Herman Melville,* 2:523. Additionally, Bulwer-Lytton's *The Pilgrims of the Rhine,* which Melville received as a gift from Mrs. Sarah Huyler Moorewood on 1 January 1854 (Merton Sealts, *Melville's Reading: A Checklist of Books Owned and Borrowed,* entry 333), resembles the anatomy and may well have served as another precedent for Melville's book and have exerted some influence upon the creation of *The Confidence-Man.* Bulwer's novel, too, concerns a river voyage and is largely given to conversations by its principal characters. There are also several interpolated stories, as in *The Confidence-Man.* Finally, the prevailing mood of *Pilgrims of the Rhine* is one of melancholy, full of lamentation for a time now past and cynicism about the present age, the "age of paper" and "the Press" as one character describes it.

15. Leyda, *Log,* 2:570.

16. William Braswell notes in *Melville's Religious Thought* (p. 81n.) that Melville marked this passage.

17. Herman Melville, *Moby-Dick,* p. 347; Herman Melville, *Pierre,* p. 212.

18. Pitch, the Missouri bachelor, may be an exception. He is not foolish; rather, in placing confidence in the P.I.O. man, he proves that he has a heart. As the cosmopolitan would later describe him to Charlie Noble, Pitch is a "genial misanthrope" whose rough exterior hides a soft heart.

19. On one of the manuscript pages of "Titles for Chapters" (which is reprinted in an appendix to the Hendricks House edition of *The Confidence-Man,* pp. 380–84), Melville had written to the side of one of the proposed chapter titles "Dedicated to victims of Auto da Fe."

20. Leyda, *Log,* 2:529.

21. Ibid., 2:508.

22. Herman Melville, *Clarel: A Poem and Pilgrimage in the Holy Land,* 2:297–98.

23. Leyda, *Log,* 2:523, 528–29.

24. *Harper's New Monthly Magazine,* November 1855, pp. 854–55. Hershel Parker has nominated the sketch "The Mystified Barber" from P. T. Barnum's *The Life of P. T. Barnum by Himself* (1855) as a possible source (Norton Critical Edition of *The Confidence-Man,* p. 264n.); and Donald Yannella, in "Source for the Diddling of William Cream in *The Confidence-Man,*" has identified a sketch entitled

"The Danger of Diddling a Barber" in Denis Corcoran's *Pickings from the Portfolio of the Reporter of the New Orleans "Picayune"* (1846) as a possible source. The parallels between "A Barberised Drama" and chapters 42 and 43, however, strike me as more compelling than either of the sources suggested by Parker and Yannella. But be that as it may, this sketch is the more credible source because it was published in a magazine that Melville subscribed to and was likely to have on hand. Both Parker and Yannella confess that there is no evidence that Melville read either Barnum or Corcoran's books. This dramatic sketch is brief and is reprinted below:

ACT FIRST

Scene: A Metropolitan Barber's Shop.
          Dramatic Persones: Oily, Jones.
Oily.   Take a seat, Sir; pray take a seat.
[Oily *puts a chair for* Jones, who sits. *During the following dialogue* Oily *continues cutting* Jones's *hair.*]
Oily.   We have had much wet, Sir.
Jones.   Very much.
Oily.   And yet October's early days were fine.
Jones.   They were.
Oily.   I hoped fair weather might have lasted us until the end.
Jones.   At *one* time, so did *I.*
Oily.   But we have had it very wet.
Jones.   We *have.*
                    [*A pause of some minutes.*
Oily.   I know not, Sir, who cut your hair last time;
          But *this* I say, Sir, it was badly cut.
          No doubt 'twas in the country?
Jones.   No—in town.
Oily.   Indeed! I should have fancied otherwise.
Jones.   'Twas cut in town—and in this very room.
Oily.   Amazement! But I now remember well:
          We had an awkward new provincial hand,
          A fellow from the country: Sir, he did
          More damage to my business in a week
          Than all my skill can in a year repair.
          He must have cut your hair.
Jones.   *(looking scrutinizingly at his interlocutor).*
          No; 'twas *yourself.*
Oily.   Myself!—impossible! You must mistake.
Jones.   I *don't* mistake: 'twas you that cut my hair.
          [*A long pause, interrupted only by the more frequent clipping of the scissors.*]
Oily.   Your hair is very dry, Sir.
Jones.   Ah!—indeed!

Oily.	Yes—*very* dry. Our *"Vegetable Extract"* moistens hair.
Jones.	I like it dry.
Oily.	But, Sir, the hair when dry, turns quickly *gray*.
Jones.	That color I prefer.
Oily.	But hair, when gray, will rapidly fall off.
	And baldness will ensue.
Jones.	I would be bald.
Oily.	Perhaps you mean to say you'd like a wig:
	We've wigs so natural they can't be told
	From real hair.
Jones.	Deception I detest.

[*Another pause ensues, during which* Oily *blows down* Jones's *neck, and relieves him from a linen wrapper, in which he has been enveloped during the process of hair-cutting.*]

Oily.	We've brushes, soaps, and scents of every kind.
Jones.	I *see* you have. (Pays a sixpence.) I think you'll
	find that right.
Oily.	Is there nothing I can show you, Sir.
Jones.	No, nothing. Yes—there may be something, too
	That you may show me.
Oily.	Name it, Sir.
Jones.	The door. [Exit Jones.
Oily.	(To his man). That's a rare customer, at any rate.
	Had I cut him as short as he cut me,
	How little hair upon his head would be!
	But, if kind friends will all our pains requite,
	We'll hope for better luck another night.

                                    [*Shop-bell rings, and curtain falls.*

    25. The discussion of punning in this dramatic sketch and Melville's barber episode relies upon Eric Partridge, ed., *A Dictionary of the Underworld*, for definitions of nineteenth-century cant terms.

    26. This expression was included in one of the alternate chapter titles for chapter 43, which was eventually shortened to "Very Charming." The revision of chapter titles is included in Foster's edition of *The Confidence-Man*, pp. 380–84. Foster believes that Melville had "difficulty" phrasing this chapter title because "the roles of man and reptile are the reverse of what he needed if he was to keep the Confidence Man pretty much in the same rank with the snake" ("Introduction," pp.lxx–lxxiii). However, it appears that William Cream was conceived as a sharper himself and therefore more of a serpent than the quixotic Goodman and that Melville was not at all confused when he wrote the chapter title.

    27. Foster, "Introduction," p. lxxxiv. However, Shroeder, in "Sources and Symbols for Melville's Confidence Man," pp. 311–12, and Daniel G. Hoffman, in *Form and Fable in American Fiction*, p. 309, have expressed the opinion that the "horned altar" of the lamp suggests

the "four horns of the altar" in Revelation 9:13–18 and the "robed man" St. John. Foster's more general interpretation of the symbolism as referring to the "light" contained in the Old and New Testaments, however, seems to me more plausible.

28. Herman Melville, *Great Short Works of Herman Melville*, ed. Warner Berthoff, p. 194.

29. Miguel de Unamuno, *Tragic Sense of Life*, pp. 95–96.

30. *Letters*, p. 132.

31. Ibid., p. 129.

Bibliography

Arvin, Newton. *Herman Melville.* New York: William Sloane Associates, 1950.

Barbour, James, and Robert Sattelmeyer. "A Possible Source and Model for 'The Story of China Aster' in Melville's *The Confidence-Man.*" *American Literature* 48 (1977): 577–83.

Bergmann, Johannes Dietrich. "The Original Confidence Man: The Development of the American Confidence Man in the Sources and Backgrounds of Herman Melville's *The Confidence-Man: His Masquerade.*" Ph.D. dissertation, University of Connecticut, 1968.

Berthoff, Warner. *The Example of Melville.* New York: W. W. Norton & Co., 1972.

_____ . "Herman Melville: *The Confidence-Man.*" In *Landmarks of American Writing,* edited by Hennig Cohen, pp. 121–33. New York: Basic Books, 1969.

Branch, Watson. "The Genesis, Composition, and Structure of *The Confidence-Man.*" *Nineteenth-Century Fiction* 27 (1973): 424–48.

_____ . "The Mute as Metaphysical Scamp." In Herman Melville, *The Confidence-Man: His Masquerade,* edited by Hershel Parker, pp. 316–19. New York: W. W. Norton & Co., 1971.

Braswell, William. *Melville's Religious Thought.* Durham: University of North Carolina Press, 1943.

Bulwer-Lytton, Edward George. *The Pilgrims of the Rhine.* London: Tilt, 1840.

Cervantes, Miguel de. *Adventures of Don Quixote de la Mancha.* Translated by Charles Jervas. 2 vols. Philadelphia: Blanchard and Lea, 1854.

Chase, Richard. "An Approach to Melville." *Partisan Review* 14 (1947): 285–94.

_____ . "Melville's Confidence Man." *Kenyon Review* 11 (1949): 122–40.

Cohen, Hennig. Introduction to *The Confidence-Man: His Masquerade,* by Herman Melville. New York: Holt, Rinehart & Winston, 1964.

Coleridge, Samuel T. *Literary Remains.* 2 vols. London: William Pickering, 1836.

Davis, Chester L. "Mark Twain's Religious Beliefs as Indicated by Notations in His Books." *The Twainian* 5 (September–October 1955) and 6 (November–December 1955): 1–4; 3–4.

Dickinson, Emily. Poem "1551." *The Complete Poems of Emily Dickinson.* Edited by Thomas H. Johnson. Boston: Little, Brown & Co., 1960.

Drew, Philip. "Appearance and Reality in Melville's *The Confidence-Man.*" *ELH* 31 (1964): 418–42.

Eberwein, Jane D. "Joel Barlow and *The Confidence-Man.*" *American Transcendental Quarterly* 24, supp. 1 (1974): 28–29.

Feidelson, Charles, Jr. *Symbolism and American Literature.* Chicago: University of Chicago Press, 1953.

Fiedler, Leslie. "Out of the Whale." *The Nation,* 19 November 1949, pp. 494–95.

Foster, Elizabeth. Introduction to *The Confidence-Man: His Masquerade,* by Herman Melville. New York: Hendricks House, 1954.

Franklin, H. Bruce. *The Wake of the Gods: Melville's Mythology.* Stanford: Stanford University Press, 1963.

Frye, Northrop. *Anatomy of Criticism: Four Essays.* Princeton: Princeton University Press, 1971.

Fuller, Roy. Introduction to *The Confidence-Man: His Masquerade,* by Herman Melville. London: John Lehmann, 1948.

Hawthorne, Nathaniel. *The House of the Seven Gables.* Columbus: Ohio State University Press, 1965.

Hayford, Harrison. "Poe in *The Confidence-Man.*" *Nineteenth-Century Fiction* 14 (1959): 207–18. Reprinted in *The Confidence-Man,* edited by Hershel Parker, pp. 344–53. New York: W. W. Norton & Co., 1971.

———. "The Significance of Melville's 'Agatha' Letters." *ELH* 12 (1946): 299–310.

Hemingway, Ernest. *Death in the Afternoon.* New York: Charles Scribner's Sons, 1932.

Hoffman, Daniel. *Form and Fable in American Fiction.* New York: Oxford University Press, 1961.

———. "Melville's 'Story of China Aster.'" *American Literature* 22 (1950): 137–49.

Howard, Leon. *Herman Melville: A Biography.* Berkeley & Los Angeles: University of California Press, 1967.

Karcher, Carolyn Lury. *Shadow Over the Promised Land: Slavery, Race, and Violence in Melville's America.* Baton Rouge: Louisiana State University Press, 1980.

_____ . "The Story of Charlemont: A Dramatization of Melville's Concepts of Fiction in *The Confidence-Man: His Masquerade.*" *Nineteenth-Century Fiction* 21 (1966): 73–84.

Keysor, Elizabeth. "'Quite an Original': The Cosmopolitan in *The Confidence-Man.*" *Texas Studies in Language and Literature* 2 (1973): 279–300.

Lang, Hans-Joachim, and Benjamin Lease. "Melville's Cosmopolitan: Bayard Taylor in *The Confidence-Man.*" *American Studies* 22 (1977): 286–89.

Levin, Harry. "'Don Quixote' and 'Moby-Dick.'" In *Cervantes Across the Centuries*, edited by Angel Flores and M. J. Bernardette, pp. 217–26. New York: Harper & Row, 1966.

Lewis, R. W. B. Afterword to *The Confidence-Man: His Masquerade*, by Herman Melville. New York: Signet, 1964.

Leyda, Jay. *The Melville Log: A Documentary Life of Herman Melville.* 2 vols. New York: Harcourt, Brace and Company, 1951.

Long, Raymond. "The Hidden Sun: A Study of the Influence of Shakespeare on the Creative Imagination of Herman Melville." Ph.D. dissertation, University of California, Los Angeles, 1965.

Magaw, Malcolm O. "*The Confidence-Man* and Christian Deity: Melville's Imagery of Ambiguity." *Explorations of Literature, Louisiana State University Studies* 18 (1966): 81–99.

Matthiessen, F. O. *American Renaissance: Art and Expression in the Age of Emerson and Whitman.* London & New York: Oxford University Press, 1941.

McCarthy, Paul. "Elements of Anatomy in Melville's Fiction." *Studies in the Novel* (North Texas State University) 6(1974): 38–61.

_____ . "The 'Soldier of Fortune' in Melville's *The Confidence-Man.*" *Emerson Society Quarterly*, no. 33 (4th Quarter 1963), 21–24.

McHaney, Thomas. "*The Confidence-Man* and Satan's Disguises in *Paradise Lost.*" *Nineteenth-Century Fiction* 30 (1975): 200–206.

Melville, Herman. *Clarel: A Poem and Pilgrimage in the Holy Land.* London: Constable & Co., 1924.

_____ . *The Collected Poems of Herman Melville*, edited by Howard P. Vincent. Chicago: Hendricks House, 1947.

_____ . *The Confidence-Man: His Masquerade.* Evanston & Chicago: Northwestern University Press and The Newberry Library, 1982.

_____ . *Great Short Works of Herman Melville*, edited by

Warner Berthoff. New York: Harper & Row, 1966.

———. "Hawthorne and His 'Mosses.'" Reprinted in *Moby-Dick*, edited by Harrison Hayford and Hershel Parker, pp. 535–51. New York: W. W. Norton & Co., 1967.

———. *The Letters of Herman Melville*, edited by Merrell R. Davis and William H. Gilman. New Haven: Yale University Press, 1960.

———. *Mardi: and a Voyage Thither*. Evanston & Chicago: Northwestern University Press and The Newberry Library, 1970.

———. *Moby-Dick: or, The Whale*, edited by Harrison Hayford and Hershel Parker. New York: W. W. Norton & Co., 1967.

———. *Pierre: or the Ambiguities*. Evanston & Chicago: Northwestern University Press and The Newberry Library, 1971.

———. *Redburn: His First Voyage*. Evanston & Chicago: Northwestern University Press and The Newberry Library, 1969.

———. *White-Jacket: or, The World in a Man-of-War*. Evanston & Chicago: Northwestern University Press and The Newberry Library, 1970.

Miller, James E., Jr. *A Reader's Guide to Herman Melville*. New York: Farrar, Straus, and Giroux, 1962.

Milton, John. *Complete Poems and Major Prose*, edited by Merritt Y. Hughes. New York: Odyssey, 1957.

Oliver, Egbert S. "Melville's Goneril and Fanny Kemble." *New England Quarterly* 18 (1945): 489–500.

———. "Melville's Picture of Emerson and Thoreau in 'The Confidence-Man.'" *College English* 8 (1946): 61–72.

Partridge, Eric, ed. *A Dictionary of the Underworld*. New York: Macmillan, 1950.

Parker, Hershel. Foreword to *The Confidence-Man: His Masquerade*, by Herman Melville. New York: W. W. Norton & Co., 1971.

———. "The Metaphysics of Indian-hating." *Nineteenth-Century Fiction* 18 (1963): 165–73. Reprinted in the Norton Critical Edition of *The Confidence-Man*, pp. 323–31.

Pearce, Roy Harvey. "Melville's Indian Hater: A Note on the Meaning of *The Confidence-Man*." *PMLA* 67 (1952): 942–48.

Pommer, Henry F. *Milton and Melville*. Pittsburgh: University of Pittsburgh Press, 1950.

Quirk, Tom. "Saint Paul's Types of the Faithful and Melville's

Confidence Man." *Nineteenth-Century Fiction* 28 (1974): 472–77.

————. "Two Sources in *The Confidence-Man.*" *Melville Society Extracts*, no. 39 (September 1979), 12–13.

Ramsey, William M. "The Moot Points of Melville's Indian-Hating." *American Literature* 52 (1980): 224–35.

Reeves, Paschal. "The 'Deaf Mute' Confidence Man: Melville's Impostor in Action." *MLN* 75 (1960): 18–20.

Sealts, Merton S. "Melville and Emerson's Rainbow." *ESQ: A Journal of the American Renaissance* 26 (1980): 53–78.

————. *Melville's Reading: A Checklist of Books Owned and Borrowed.* Madison, Milwaukee, and London: University of Wisconsin Press, 1966.

Shakespeare, William. *The Riverside Shakespeare.* Boston: Houghton Mifflin Co., 1974.

Shroeder, John. "Sources and Symbols for Melville's *Confidence-Man.*" *PMLA* 66 (1951): 363–80. Reprinted in *The Confidence-Man,* edited by Hershel Parker, pp. 298–316. New York: W. W. Norton & Co., 1971.

Smith, Paul. "*The Confidence-Man* and the Literary World of New York." *Nineteenth-Century Fiction* 16 (1962): 329–37.

Thompson, Lawrance. *Melville's Quarrel with God.* Princeton: Princeton University Press, 1952.

Trimpi, Helen. "Three of Melville's Confidence Men: William Cullen Bryant, Theodore Parker, and Horace Greeley." *Texas Studies in Literature and Language* 21 (1979): 368–95.

Unamuno, Miguel de. *Tragic Sense of Life.* Translated by J. E. Crawford Flitch. New York: Dover Publications, 1954.

Viardot, Louis. Introduction to *Don Quixote de la Mancha,* by Miguel de Cervantes. Philadelphia: Blanchard and Lea, 1853.

Van Vechten, Carl. "The Later Work of Herman Melville." *The Double Dealer* 3 (1922): 9–20. Parts reprinted in *The Confidence-Man,* edited by Hershel Parker, p. 283. New York: W. W. Norton & Co., 1971.

Weissbuch, Ted N. "A Note on the Confidence-Man's Counterfeit Detector." *Emerson Society Quarterly,* no. 19 (2nd Quarter 1960), 16–18.

Wright, Nathalia. *Melville's Use of the Bible.* Durham, N.C.: Duke University Press, 1949.

Yannella, Donald. "Source for the Diddling of William Cream in *The Confidence-Man.*" *American Transcendental Quarterly* 17 (1967): 22–23.

Index